YORK UNIVERSITY   ATKINSON COLLEGE
GEOGRAPHICAL MONOGRAPHS

Residential Satisfaction and

rban Environmental Preferences

Frederick Ermuth

geographical   monographs

no.3,1974

I.S.B.N.   0-919604-10-2

Department of Geography /Atkinson College/ York University,
Downsview, Ontario, Canada M3J 2R7

**dedicated to
michele, roger,
and christine**

ACKNOWLEDGMENTS

Conducting this investigation and writing this report were intellectualy satisfying experiences largely because so many persons were generous with their time, knowledge and advice.

I am particularly indebted to Professor Frank E. Horton, and to the other members of my doctoral dissertation advisory committee; to Professor Gerard Rushton, for broaching several challenging ideas which contributed to the clarity and scope of this work, to Professors Kenneth Dueker, Clyde Kohn, James Lindberg and Neil Salisbury, all of the Department of Geography, University of Iowa, for providing many constructive suggestions and for offering reassurance on the merits of the study.

Professor Larry Landis, Department of Sociology, Drake University, provided considerable stimulus to my thought and to a crystallization of ideas which form the basis of the chapter on the theoretical dimensions of residential satisfaction. His substantial methodological advice broadened my understanding of the problem.

Finally, the financial support of the following two organizations was appreciated. The computational costs at the University of Iowa's Computer Center's IBM 360/65 were, in part, paid for by a Computer Research Grant of the Graduate College and, under a research contract, by the Central Iowa Regional Planning Commission, Des Moines, Iowa. The Planning Commission also made freely available to me the data used in the analyses. The data was originally collected in 1971 for a Des Moines Housing and Attitude Survey, under the auspices of Mr. T. Urban.

TABLE OF CONTENTS

LIST OF TABLES

LIST OF FIGURES

CHAPTER I

INTRODUCTION

The Research Problem

Imperfect knowledge of consumer preferences for housing
represents an important obstacle to the understanding of change
in the residential spatial structure. The paucity of information on relevant factors involved in the choice of a dwelling-
unit and a residential environment has resulted in models of
residential satisfaction and choice that do not adequately
replicate urban reality. Efforts to improve urban residential
quality assume that research can distinguish good from bad
neighborhoods and can isolate specific features that are related
to overall quality. An environment of high quality may be
defined as one that conveys a sense of well being and satisfaction to its population through values that may be (1) physical,
such as accessibility to essential facilities and good means of
spatial mobility, (2) non-utilitarian amenities, and (3) social
and symbolic values such as status, pretige, autonomy, socia-
bility and sense of identity. Because widespread resistance to
planning proposals exist, see Fried and Gleicher, (1961), it
appears that research should shift from the almost exclusive
concern of planners' intuitive estimates of the needs, desires
and preferences of the public and the ways of realizing these

1

assumed values to the prior problem of discovering what the preferences are.

In order to understand man's perception and cognitive structuring of the social and physical residential structure, analysis of information on attitudes, values, neighborhoods, and life-styles is an essential prerequisite. While recent studies have begun to investigate the relationship of man and his social behavior to the environment more carefully than in the past, literature in this research area is fragmented and unsystematic. An explicit formulation of the question is mostly absent although occasionally implicit assumptions concerning the kinds of relationships considered appropriate can be identified. The primary emphasis of this literature is on social variables which are thought to be related to the urban environment, such as social rank or status (Beshers, 1962), life-style (Bell, 1958) and value orientation (Seeley, et. al., 1956).

A fundamental motivation for the research whose findings are presented below is that the quantitative measures of preferences for different factors of a residential environment should ultimately be relevant to some of today's pressing questions of the 'most desirable' or 'least desirable' forms of metropolitan growth. Determining the desirability of a residential environment is clearly a difficult task because it is difficult to state what constitutes a 'decent home' and a 'suitable living environment'?

A fruitful approach to the problem is an explicit examination of preferences[1] for attributes of the urban residential environment[2] that contribute to a household's residential satisfaction. Admittedly, residential satisfaction is only one aspect of the complex set of relationships involved in the residential location process. But, its significance has been attested to by the conceptualizations of the residential location decision by Rees (1970), Brown and Moore (1970) and the empirical work of Rossi (1955), Lansing and Barth (1964), and many other researchers. Indeed, Boyce (1969, p. 22) notes that "residential change appears to be highly voluntary, (i.e., strictly speaking, unnecessary) and to be triggered by discontent with the present neighborhood or house. The basic force seems to be 'push' rather than a 'pull' feature..."

Research must thus establish the relative priorities of urban environmental attributes as they contribute to current residential satisfaction, or dissatisfaction. Are social

---

[1]The term 'preference' indicates some relative weighting of desirability of alternative residential attributes.

[2]Urban residential environment is defined as a collection or combination of attributes, or characteristics; such as the house, the lot, and social, physical and esthetic neighborhood considerations.

factors of the environment more important than physical or esthetic factors? Do households in different sub-areas of the metropolitan area view housing quality, and the social life of a community differently? How important are spatial factors, such as accessibility considerations and relative location of the sub-area within the whole urban area? Also, to what extent do households trade-off and substitute one factor for another?

It is hypothesized that different people perceive and evaluate the same segment of the urban residential environment differently (Lee, 1969). Two logical questions arise from this simple hypothesis. How do these perceptions and evaluations differ? And what factors explain the variation? Answers to these questions are complicated by the fact that persons often have difficulty in articulating ideas associated with their perception and evaluation of urban residential factors. Perceptions vary not only by going from one specific residential characteristic to another but change also with changes in one's attitudes, expectations, his needs, and values.

To be comprehensive, therefore, research must not be limited to the identification of housing preferences and the estimation of their relative importance. It must also focus on variations in the characteristics of households and variations of attributes of the social and physical environment.

4

This quantitative assessment of residential satisfaction has theoretical implications as well as potential practical applications for planning agencies. If a household's preferences for attributes of a residence and a residential environment were more fully understood, and if this understanding could be extended from individuals to aggregates of identifiable groups of households with similar preferences then we could add to our ability to construct usable models of urban growth. In the aggregate, the reasons why people chose a residential location and, more specifically, what attributes contribute to residential satisfaction determine, to a large degree, the way in which cities grow. The research reported here provides some of this necessary data for more ambitious modeling. For the Central Iowa Regional Planning Commission this research provides explicit information about which residential environmental attributes are most preferred and the trade-offs between attributes for identified subgroups of the total population. For instance, a household may desire both accessibility to work, and a spacious lot on a quiet street. But, one of these attributes often may have to be selected at the expense of the other. The household will have made, one assumes, a subjectively optimum compromise in its housing choice. Given accurate knowledge of such trade-offs for the identified population subgroups the planning process could systematically incorporate the preferences and seek to provide a 'subjectively optimum environment' on the basis of this empirically derived quantitative-qualitative description and assessment of what this environment means to the persons who live in it. More realistically, the planners may wish to modify this environment on the basis of desirable societal goals, anticipated temporal changes in the preferences, and subject to such constraints as income and available land.

Brief Outline of Literature Related to this Problem

Housing preferences could conceivably be elicited by interviewing home buyers, realtors or contractors. The choice of the appropriate group should logically be based on a comparison of information accuracy and cost. Prestemon's (1969) exploratory study of Des Moines, Iowa, investigates the relative merits of the three groups and tentatively concludes that builders and, or, realtors accurately reflect consumer preferences for some housing characteristics but do not completely perceive other preferences. Hence a more complete definition of housing preferences can be realized by interviewing home buyers directly.

A great many studies have been concerned with the measurement of preferences generally for limited and isolated factors of the housing environment, sometimes in 'artificial' contexts (Rossi, 1955; Michelson, 1966; Peterson, 1967). This is done to build up a more rigorous methodology and theoretical basis for future applications in the real world. Another research category approaches the measurement problem of housing preferences through the identification, isolation and measurement of a much wider range of factors assumed to be involved in human decision-making and then investigates their relationship to the urban residential environment (Wilson, 1962, Hoinville, 1971).

The few selected references were chosen because they are indicative and representative of the diverse methodological approaches to the research problem, and because their empirical findings were examined and evaluated in the design of this research.

Michelson (1966) attempts to shed light on the systematic association of social variables and an 'ideal' physical environment. His data points out two elements of social diversity in the population as prominent for planning physical aspects of the city; value orientation and the nature and extent of social interaction. The fact that he used only 75 respondents in his interview survey, however, make his conclusions tentative. But they offer intriguing avenues for further investigations, partially to be pursued in the research reported here.

Peterson (1967) in a study which supports the speculative hypothesis 'that the desirability of the visual appearance of residential neighborhoods is a multidimensional phenomenon that can best be simplified by an orthogonal model of preference'

(p. 29), uses 23 color photos to simulate visual apperance. He

finds that the most significant dimensions are general physical

quality, reflected by the perceived age of the neighborhood and

'harmony with nature', possibly a reflection of cultural condi-

tions. The originality of methodology and speculative con-

clusions on the implications of his findings are most interesting.

While slides indicate only static aspects of the visual environ-

ment, Petersons' study shows that esthetic considerations must

be included in a comprehensive investigation of housing prefer-

ences.

Rossi (1955), while focussing his research specifically

on residential relocation, provides informative insights and

selected empirical evidence on housing preferences in terms of

the characteristics of the dwelling-unit and its immediate social

and economic environment. Subsequently, a number of researchers,

for example Lansing and Barth (1964), attempt to explain resi-

dential movement and confirm many aspects of Rossi's work on

preferences, often solely in terms of sociological variables and

in an essentially aspatial context.

Perhaps the most widely known study was completed by

Wilson (1962). He analyzed 'livability' factors of two cities

defined as the sum total of the qualities of the urban environ-

ment which induce satisfaction in a resident. In addition, he

devises a 'standard' technique of analysis of the attitudes of an urban population with his pilot study of the Crescent Cities in North Carolina. While there are many conceptually appealing features of his technique his reliance on a hypothetical problem situation in which people were asked to 'daydream' about an ideal city and in a gaming situation specify likes and dislikes for given urban features does not appear particularly suited for a realistic identification of basic dimensions contributing to residential satisfaction.

Hoinville (1971) seeks to refine and extend the methodology developed in the Crescent Cities.

> The starting point for this research was the need to understand trade-off preferences. The general direction of preference is already known. . .
> The major problem lies both in the reconciliation of conflicting preferences and--given limited investment resources--in the identification of relative priorities. (p. 39)

Hoinville's 'Priority Evaluation Method' permits the derivation of a value of amenity loss (or gain) arising from a planning decision. However, since the method can not handle the interdependencies which are known to exist between the considered variables and poses to the respondents alternative trade-off situations which are exceedingly hypothetical and unreal, any derived value of amenity loss is a quantity of unknown reliability.

An alternative and more fruitful approach is that utilized in a national survey conducted by the Highway Research Board on 'Moving Behavior and Residential Choice' (HRB, 1969). The

survey which interviewed 1476 households in 43 cities, varying in
size from Los Angeles, Detroit and Boston to Utica, N.Y., Amarillo,
Tex., and Bakersfield, Calif., is especially useful if viewed
as a delineation of a range of overall, national preferences. It
provides a frame of reference for identifying housing preferences
in a particular metropolitan area. A crucial assumption of the
HRB study, adopted for this research, is that housing and environmental preferences can be inferred from the current residential
experience, based on present housing accommodation and expressed
satisfactions.

Most of the literature provides justification of the
utility of questionnaire survey data to derive housing preferences. It also outlines the variety and range of housing and
environmental factors which may be considered relevant by households, in their decision-making, and, therefore, will have to be
incorporated into a comprehensive empirical analysis.

With regard to the selection of an appropriate research
methodology the preference literature is characterized by
great diversity and provides little guidance. However, an
effective and theoretically meaningful methodology to investigate the research problem was readily found in the literature
that deals with attitude measurement in psychology (Ramsay and
Case, 1970). Shinn (1972) in a methodological paper very
recently corroborated independently the approach taken here.

One final aspect of the illucidation of housing preferences, as developed in the literature, needs clarification. The HRB study dealt with only current as opposed to future housing preferences, or with 'hypothetical-ideal' situations of how households perceive and evaluate housing and neighborhood features. At this stage of analysis of housing preferences a focus on current preferences must be considered of major importance because of a higher degree of factual reliability. This does not mean that the other approaches are less valuable. Indeed, they appear to be complementary in a better understanding of housing preferences. However, paraphrasing Hoinville's (1971) comments on the difficulties in extending the role of social survey investigations beyond the measurement of facts and behavior it becomes clear that hypothetically phrased preference questions asked of those without knowledge and experience of the alternatives may not provide useful or reliable answers.

Study Area and Data

This research is based on an areally stratified random sample of the metropolitan Des Moines households. The sample includes 778 households in the City of Des Moines, divided into 12 areas, and in the four contiguous western suburbs of Urbandale, West Des Moines, Clive and Windsor Heights. Figure 1 shows the metropolitan study area and the areal subdivisions.

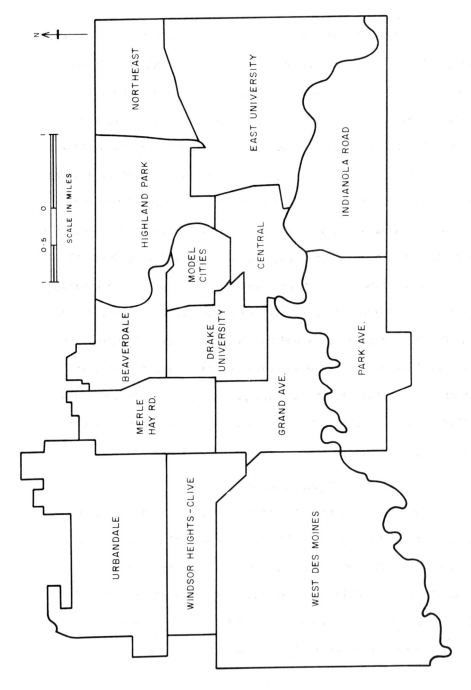

FIGURE 1: THE METROPOLITAN DES MOINES, IOWA, STUDY AREA

The Des Moines metropolitan area is particularly appropriate for this study of current residential satisfaction. It is characterized by very slow rates of change in population composition and growth. This should increase the reliability and stability of the identified preferences for housing environment attributes.

The data was gathered for a 'Housing and Attitude Survey' of the Central Iowa Regional Planning Commission, Des Moines, Iowa, in 1970. Details of the sample design and a copy of the questionnaire can be found in Appendix A.

The survey elicited the socio-economic and demographic characteristics of each household, such as income, age, size, and composition of the family and length of residency at the current address. In addition, three well known sociological attitude scales, each consisting of a series of questions which are assumed to measure the same underlying attitudinal continuum, were modified to permit the derivation of three dimensions which are meaningful indicators of residential satisfaction. They attempt to measure (1) the extent of social interaction patterns of a household within his neighborhood, (2) the strength of local territorial identification of a respondent, and (3) the degree of isolation that a household feels toward his neighborhood.[1] Finally, a series of 22 direct questions ascertained a household's perceptions of specific building aspects and of environmental factors.

Most of the respondents' subjective statements regarding housing attributes are in categorical form, i.e., on a scale of 1 - 5. Given the need for intervally scaled data for the statistical analyses it was necessary to transform the response data. A scaling technique, based on Thurstone's 'Law of Categorical Judgment', as adapted and modified by Torgerson (1958) and Peterson (1965) accomplished this. The specific computer program for this methodology was written by Wachs (1967). In essence the technique makes the data continuous on the basis of 'Z-scores'. The use of 'Z-scores' is satisfactory, since the original responses to an attribute over 778 individuals were found to be normally distributed (see also Shinn, 1970, p. 49).

Research Statement and Objectives

The basic research premise is that the satisfaction of a household with the housing it chose and is currently occupying, as reflected in responses to questions toward the multi-attribute dwelling-unit and residential environment, can be employed to

---

[1]The concept of neighborhood is consistently used in this research as defined by Warren (1963, p. 9): A spatially localized social system that is integrated by means of families and cooperation (see Chapter II).

make statements about housing preferences. A households' satisfaction with a given urban residential environment is affected
not only by the attributes of the dwelling-unit but, it is also
affected by accessibility to essential facilities and amenities,
by symbolic values such as status and prestige of, and sense of
identity with the environment, as well as socio-economic characteristics of the household.

The ex post facto housing choice behavior of a household,
therefore, is conceptualized as being based upon a revealed subjective preference scaling of all possible housing and residential
environment opportunities. Given a particular housing choice of
a household these preferences are assumed to be a function of
his perception and evaluation of relevant urban environmental
characteristics.

Assume that an urban environment is conceptualized by a
household as occupying a position in 'perceived space' which is
based on a household's perception of those attributes which he
uses to make discrimination judgments. It is these perceived
dimensions in contrast to an 'objective' description of the
environment in physical, social and economic terms that are relevant from the viewpoint of consumer housing satisfaction. More-
over, households may differentially weight perceived housing
dimensions in terms of their relative importance in an evaluative
context. Satisfaction thus reflects the differential saliences

and particular combination of values which an individual household applies to the housing characteristics of interest.

Social Psychologists' research indicates that all that man learns throughout his life depends on the effective operation of his five senses, and ultimately, on his cumulative experiences (Sartain, 1958; Fishbein, 1967). The perceived reaction of a person to a particular environmental stimulus, therefore, can be viewed as a result of the operation of his senses at that particular point in space and time as modified by his cumulative lifetime experiences. Based on the sensitivity of the person to the intensity, quality and duration of the sensation evoked by the environmental stimulus, and received by the five senses, the individual experiences feelings that lead to the establishment of an affective value, that is, a degree of satisfaction. As time passes an individual's feelings about such a subjective experience leads to the formation of attitudes, motives and habits. Sartain (1958, p. 81) defines an attitude as a latent behavioral disposition to become motivated with respect to an object; the residential environment.

Motives and attitudes involve a human valuation process which express appreciation toward attributes of the residential environment. Value theorists suggest that value and the feeling of value are the same thing, (see Atkisson and Robinson, 1969, p. 182-183). Consequently, attitudes may be determinants of preferences among attributes of the residential environment held by individuals. Since fulfillment of motives is usually pleasant, feelings and attitudes thus are related to motivation and to economic behavior, i.e. choice of a house.

The notable psychologist Maslow (1964) identifies a continuum of man's motives which he then develops into an ascending hierarchy beginning with those physiological needs related to man's need for food, shelter, safety and security, progressing through social needs related to belonging, associating and acceptance, to external ego needs relating to status, respect, appreciation and favorable regard and internal ego needs relating to self-confidence, self-esteem, achievement and knowledge and culminating with those needs related to self-fulfillment which involve the maximum use of all of man's resources. Maslow emphasizes that the satisfaction of lower level needs leads to a reduction in their motivational power and to a re-orientation of motives around the achievement of higher order satisfactions.

In the context of an individual's residential satisfaction it would appear that environmental attributes are related to the fulfillment of social and ego needs. This assumes that more basic, lower order needs are also being satisfied.

Clearly some compromise is necessary to apply this behavioral scheme to the large numbers of people living in the

Des Moines metropolitan area and still keep the analyses
economical in cost and time, and to reflect data realities. The
simplification is achieved largely through aggregation of individuals into groups that share to a large degree a similar
perceptual viewpoint of residential attributes. In making these
aggregations it is necessary to shift one's thinking from a
unique situation tied to one person to looking at a 'typical'
process associated with a particular class of people. Thus,
instead of dealing with actual persons, the intent is to define
preferences that differentiate between archetypes in the population.

The research strategy for the investigation of urban
residential satisfaction as a function of environmental preferences and household characteristics can best be understood
by referring to Figure 2. Since the total research effort
progresses sequentially it has been categorized into six major
stages in the flow-chart. Each of these research stages is
composed of smaller analytical steps.[1]

The overall objective is to derive empirically valid
statement about group housing preferences which can form postulates in a theory of residential satisfaction and, ultimately,

---

[1]The specific computer programs to accomplish the analyses
are described in Wittick and Horton (1968).

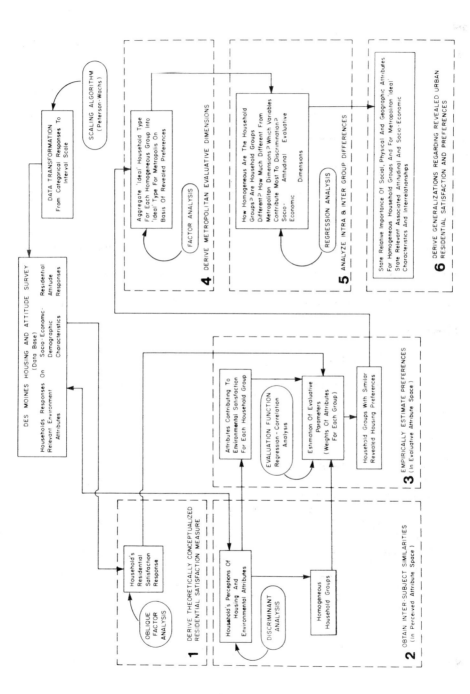

FIGURE 2: RESEARCH STRATEGY FOR THE ANALYSIS OF URBAN RESIDENTIAL SATISFACTION

provide input to our knowledge of residential choice behavior.
The statements will explicate the relative preferences of households for social, physical, spatial and esthetic aspects of
the residential environment and provide a quantitative - qualitative assessment of current residential satisfaction (stage 6).
This necessitates investigation of the relationships between the
residential satisfaction of households, their perception and
evaluation of relevant factors of residences as a function of
variations in their socio-economic characteristics and of variations of attributes of the environment (see also discussion above,
p. 3-6). These relationships are indicated by the arrows in the
flow-chart.

The first research stage derives a theoretically conceptualized measure of an individual household's overall residential
satisfaction through an Oblique Factor Analysis of 19 interrelated household attitudinal responses. Aggregating the resulting three basic dimensions, and thereby relating a household's
degree of spatial identification, its relative isolation and its
social interaction patterns yields a composite index of residential
satisfaction for each separate household.

The second stage obtains inter-subject similarities. The
satisfaction of a household with the housing it chose and is
currently occupying is expressed in subjective responses to
questions regarding the dwelling-unit and residential environ-

ment. These psychological responses will be used to aggregate individuals into household groups with substantially homogeneous perceptual viewpoints (Green, 1970, p. 97). A Multiple Discriminant Analysis validates the aggregation of households into groups that are characterized by similarity of perceptual viewpoints.

The third stage empirically estimates the preferences and appropriate attribute dimensions which are viewed as salient by the household groups in making overall ratings of the respective multi-attribute residential environments (Dawes, 1964). Specifically, a multiplicative model is used to estimate the evaluative parameters of the attributes, represented by the standardized regression coefficients, for each household group. The dependent variable is the derived measure of residential satisfaction. It reflects the household's state of knowledge and beliefs about the neighborhood but does not include an evaluative dimension (Ramsay and Case, 1970, p. 185).

The next step derives evaluative dimensions for the metropolitan area population as a whole. This is done by aggregating the idea or 'typical' household type of each group into a 'typical' type for the metropolis on the basis of the revealed preferences. The specific methodology and technique selected to accomplish this is a Factor Analysis of the standardized coefficients.

The fifth research stage analyzes intra- and inter-group differences. The heterogeneity of the 'homogeneous' household

21

groups is investigated by focussing on selected processes of inter-personal influence and statistically estimating their importance. Inter-group differences in revealed preferences are identified by reference to the metropolitan norm.

CHAPTER II

MEASURING URBAN RESIDENTIAL SATISFACTION

The Theoretical Dimensions of Residential Satisfaction

A household's complex set of beliefs and expectations forms the premise for its perception and evaluation of housing environment factors and thus underly its preferences (Smith, 1969, p. 60). An understanding of the relationship between a household's informational context (beliefs, expectations, etc.) and direction of its expressed or revealed preferences is possible only in terms of the values activating a household's overall view of the housing environment. The holding of a value, say local territorial identification, sensitizes the individual to perceive and process information that pertains to it. A household which expresses a high degree of identification with a local territory, possibly reinforced by strong social interaction patterns may consider different environmental factors as relevant to its satisfaction than a 'cosmopolitan' household, which identifies to a larger extent with the metropolitan area as a whole and is less aware of local issues and problems.

Fried and Gleicher (1961) found from an interview survey that persons experienced satisfaction from living in a territory based on their strong sense of identity to local places, as well as from close associations among local people. Festinger et. al.

23

(1950) have shown that groups influence one's attitudes and actions - hence his perception process. These group pressures are transmitted through communication, a point which Deutsch (1966) emphasizes by stressing the interdependency between information flow and social cohesion in a given area. Strauss (1961, p. 67) aptly summarizes by stating that "the various kinds of urban perspectives held by residents of a city are constructed from spatial representations resulting from memberships in particular social worlds."

Consequently, a household's satisfaction with a particular urban residential neighborhood cannot be understood in isolation of the broader societal phenomenon of communal organizations (Homans, 1950; Warren, 1963; Hillery, 1968; Landis, 1971). Indeed, neighborhood satisfaction is a function in which the two dimensions of communal organizations, the vertical and the horizontal, as developed by Warren (1963), and, similarly described as the formal and communal aspects by Hillery (1968) and developed in terms of a trilogy of space, integration and cooperation, are operative.

Hillery's research leads him to develop a typology of human groups. In it, a neighborhood is identified as a communal organization with relatively low degrees of institutionalization and goal orientation, and a minimum of inclusiveness relative to smaller social units and systems, but performing major social

24

functions that have locality reference (Hillery, 1968, p. 150-151).
Warren's (1963, p. 9) definition of a neighborhood, as a spatially
localized social system that is integrated by means of families
and cooperation, appears to be in agreement.

Warren (1963) develops insights into the elusive linkages
and relations of neighborhood social system units to other social
systems. His conceptual tools are the vertical and the horizontal
patterns (Warren, 1963, p. 161).

A neighborhood's vertical pattern is the structural and
functional relations of its various social units and subsystems
to extra-neighborhood systems. The term vertical is used to
reflect the fact that such relationships often involve different
hierarchical levels within the extra-neighborhood system's
structure of power and authority. A neighborhood's horizontal.
pattern is the structural and functional relations of its
various social units and subsystems to each other. The term
horizontal is used to indicate that the neighborhood units,
insofar as their relevance to the neighborhood system, tend to
be on approximately the same hierarchical level.

In effect, there is a substantial congruence between
Hillery's communal organization and Warren's horizontal pattern
and between formal organizations and the vertical pattern,
because both stress space, integration and cooperation as important variables. Landis' research (1971) substantiates this

interpretation, as does McKinney (1966) when he writes about the so-called 'typological tradition' and such commonly used concepts as 'cosmpolitan' and 'local' (Merton, 1957).

In summary, neighborhoods are groups and social systems and parts of social systems as well. As in all groups, interaction, competition and cooperation, and integration are central to the continuing existence of the system (Homans, 1950). To understand the phenomenon of neighborhood adequately, both basic and fundamental forms of relations must be taken into consideration. A neighborhood has a horizontal (communal) aspect and a vertical (formal) aspect. For analytical purposes they can be viewed independently but to understand the nature of neighborhood it is necessary to view both.

Hillery (1968) presents a theoretical strategy for analysis and elaboration with the three key foci that are integrators of neighborhood, and hence indicators of residential satisfaction: space, family and cooperation. The following discussion will develop these key concepts in terms of the local territorial identification by households, their social interaction patterns within and degree of isolation from a neighborhood. It is noted that these indicators of residential satisfaction may well not be the only, nor necessarily the most efficient factors, but if other indicators are used the results would presumably be basically the same (Landecker, 1950).

Local Territorial Identification

Hillery suggests that all communal organizations are integrated by space, and that this process of integration is evident in spatial patterning. This concern for space as part of communal organizations, explicitly or implicitly, is widespread.[1] The problematic aspect of delineating urban-areas (neighborhoods) still remains, naturally. It can be argued that neighborhoods are distributed over a given metropolitan area in accord with rational principles, based on such concepts as time, space and distance, and economies of scale (see, for instance, Christaller, (1933). But since 'locality relevant functions' can be carried on with greater effectiveness and efficiency when they are concentrated, the households, groups and associations form, therefore, neighborhoods. This makes it

---

[1]Hall (1969) and others have written of spatial relations in terms of proxemics and Ardrey (1966) argues for what he calls the 'territorial imperative' in man. Hall, for instance, states that there are specific zones of personal space, concentric in their general orientation, and through variable from person to person, they range from zones of intimate distance, zones of personal distance and zones of social distance to zones of public distance. Lyman and Scott argue that territoriality is a neglected dimension. It is defined as an attempt to control space. They call it a fundamental human activity, and define four types of territory which are more generalized than Hall's; public territories, home territories, interactional territories and body territories. These concepts provide a reasonably sound, though admittedly speculative basis for communal neighborhood organization.

now possible to conceptualize and locate neighborhoods in terms
of unique time and space coordinates; thereby magnifying the
horizontal or communal aspects.

The smaller neighborhoods, as well as larger, metropolitan
communities, may be considered as more or less self-sufficient
systems of action, and are subject to analysis as such. The
relationship between these communities may be thought of in terms
of subordinate and superordinate -- the smallest among them is
related to the greatest in a dependency relationship. The sub-
units of the total metropolitan urban system are independent and
interdependent. The concern is to relate urban neighborhoods to
each other and to the metropolitan community (see also Dobriner,
1970, and Boskoff, 1970).[1]

In this research the metropolitan sub-area boundaries are
based on the Des Moines planners' evaluation of what local residents may perceive as neighborhoods tempered with the arbitrary
need for comparability of sub-areas and availability of statistical
data. As a result of this attempt at standardization, census
tracts were aggregated into sub-areas. This is considered adequate

---

[1]These notions relating to the vertical and horizontal
patterns of Warren (1963) were also well developed, albeit in
a different context, by Christaller (1933) in his concepts of
hierarchy and range of a good.

28

for the analysis of residential satisfaction since our theoretical framework provides the necessary guidance in choosing a model which allows to take these problems into consideration, i.e. there is no substitute for knowing that which you want to measure.

There is further justification for the adequacy of the sub-area delineation. There are two separate dimensions of space reflected in communal organizations. There is geographic space, but there is also social or symbolic space. The same kind of space, for example, Hall refers to in his study of proxemics -- the space that is a function of culture. This social space has a vertical dimension and is superimposed over horizontal or geographical space. Thus we cannot assume that a given metropolitan sub-area is, instead, since individual human beings are involved, the area became and is evolving. The very existence of community, the location of city and suburbs are functions of man living in communities. The interaction between these communities produce this new dimension of space.

Social Interaction Patterns and Degree of Isolation

A second focus which functionally integrates communal organizations in Hillery's model is the family. It is both a unit of integration and an integrating unit. Families are, at a minimum, economic units, units of stratification, and effective units of socialization. Families are conceptualized as being communal in their organizational patterns and are placed in the same model category as neighborhoods. Since a family is characterized as a social group that is limited in its inclusiveness, is highly institutionalized and is lacking an orientation toward a specific goal, it is a potential building block for the more generalized forms of communal, or formal, organizations. In fact, Hillery (1970, p. 55) argues that it is the family household which "Integrates persons into the city who would not otherwise be integrated." The family as a residential group provides for mutual, and for intra- and inter- neighborhood linkages, e.g. social interaction, for property maintenance and other functions which integrate an urban neighborhood. See Landis (1971) for a detailed synthesis of sociological research that appears to support the above argument.

Cooperation, like the foci of space and family is a necessary, though not sufficient indicator of residential satisfaction in an urban neighborhood. It also is expressed in terms of an ideal-typical model by Hillery (1970).

Naturally, a group of households does not become a neighborhood community simply by living in spatial proximity with one another. Cooperation in a community is best understood in terms of normative exchange as a result of unity, dependency, mutual aid and reciprocity -- each of which suggests a degree of interactional symmetry (Landis, 1971). In other words, to the degree that locations, definitions of the situation (residential satisfaction) and expectations are mutually shared and desired, behavior will be 'normative' and cooperation will be maximized. Cooperation coordinates and integrates the efforts of all within the group. It not only integrates, but it unifies, it functions to create and maintain dependencies and has its basis in reciprocal interaction (Homans, 1950, p. 112-113).

Meeker's (1971) recent work on decision making and exchange furthers our understanding of the processes at work. He argues that it is useful to define human societal behavior, such as residential satisfaction, as a function of the premises that actors in a given situation hold.

These premises include (1) his values, (2) his perception of the alternative behaviors available to him, (3) his expectations of the consequences of these alternatives to himself and others (consequences including the probable responses of others), and (4) a 'decision rule', which is a kind of social norm telling him how the first three premises should be combined to yield a prescription for his behavior (Meeker, 1971, p. 485).

The key for analysis seems to be the utilization of the decision-making rules. Meeker's argument and hypotheses are based on the presumption that the patterns of exchange, which are based on one or more of the following exchange rules: rationality, reciprocity, altruism, status consistency, or competition, may be found in the normative definition of the situation that is subscribed to by the social participants in the inter-action arena. Exchange rules, in other words, are norms that provide the basis for the broader concepts of cooperation and mutual aid, given a commonly held definition of the situation.

With the formation of a neighborhood community, there emerges a specific set of rules, which are more or less clearly recognized and accepted by the members of that group. They are based on a more or less commonly held set of values or beliefs. These rules provide for the basis for cooperative interaction. They provide the basis for the establishment and maintenance of the phenomenon here defined as residential satisfaction.

In summary, residential satisfaction is an emergent phenomenon, and its character at any given point in time and space, is the product of the quantity and quality of interaction along the horizontal and vertical axes of the urban system. The theoretical framework suggests that three foci, space, integration, and cooperation are necessary to describe residential satisfaction in an urban area. What remains to be done is to find suitable operational measures for these basic theoretical dimensions of residential satisfaction that affect the percep-tions and evaluations by households of specific factors of the urban residential environment.

Derivation of Residential Satisfaction Measure
for Individual Households

One of the difficulties of this research is that for the theoretical concept of residential satisfaction advocated in the last section no single, direct and operational definition can be obtained or defended. One existing approach to this special problem of survey research is the use of several different indicators, generally combined into a composite index, to represent the underlying theoretical concept (Curtis and Jackson, 1962, p. 195). The advantages of such an approach are based on the fact that additional indicators provide additional information. The composite index may increase the empirical variability of the measures to be related, thereby possibly permitting a more detailed and precise analysis. Or, the index may represent the theoretical concept, even when the individual component indicators do not. Curtis and Jackson (1962, p. 197) clarify the position of several indicators vis-a-vis the underlying theoretical concept.

> Each indicator is (1) a unique representation of some aspect of the concept, (2) a corepresentative along with other indicators of the same concept, (3) a variable which may be related to the other indicators of the same concept quite apart from their common link to that concept. and (4) a variable in its own right a part of the variation of which cannot be accounted for by either the concept or the other indicators of the concept.

These features make the use of 'multiple indicators' well
suited to the empirical analysis of residential satisfaction.
While there are serious limits to the kinds of attitudinal
data obtainable from interviews the study includes information
on 19 related attitudinal questions. The questions were derived
from three well-known sociological scales attempting to measure
the following three concepts, (1) social interaction patterns,
a modified Seashore Group Cohesiveness Scale (Miller, 1970);
(2) the degree of isolation from, or lack of integration with,
the neighborhood, a modified Srole's (1956) Anomia Scale; and
(3) the degree of local spatial identification, a modified
Glaser's (1963) Cosmopolitan-Local Scale. For details see the
data description and the questionnaire in Appendix A.

These three dimensions relating to a household's social
interaction patterns, local territorial identification and degree
of isolation, taken together, are assumed to be representative
of the three theoretical concepts of cooperation, space and family,
and, of overall residential satisfaction.[1] Urban residential
satisfaction, therfore, is used here as an indirect measure of

---

[1]But, clearly, this does not mean that these foci are
sufficient to describe all residential satisfaction variation
within an urban area. However, the literature, especially
Landecker's (1950) comparison of concepts give reason to believe
that these concepts are better than adequate.

the general factors of a neighborhood as a place to live. It
reflects the household's state of knowledge and beliefs about the
neighborhood but does not include an evaluative dimension. This
is crucial to the methodology which, in evaluative attribute
space, derives the preferences for specific factors of the
housing and residential environment (see Chapter III).

In an attempt to operationalize the residential satisfaction concept, an oblique factor analysis was performed on the
19 separate attitude questions. Rummel (1970, p. 388) advocates
oblique over orthogonal rotations on two grounds. First, it
generates additional information from the analysis since the
clusters of variables are better defined, and there is less
possibility of confusion as to the central or nuclear members
of the cluster because they are identified by high loadings on
that relevant factor. Relatedly, oblique rotations provide
information about correlations between the factors and thus
enable the researcher to assess the degree to which the data
approximates orthogonal factors. A second justification of
oblique rotations is based on epistomological grounds. Cattell
(1952, p. 309) argues that phenomena, whether singly or in
clusters, are interrelated and that therefore the world cannot
be treated realistically if the basic functional entities
represented by the factors are uncorrelated. Instead, the
factors themselves must reflect this reality. Since oblique

rotation allows this reality to be represented by the factor correlations it was selected for the analyses of the attitudinal information.

The three newly derived attitude factors are each composed of a number of strongly correlated attitude questions, providing dimensions of residential satisfaction that are considered meaningful in substantive terms as well as statistically distinct and significant (see Table 1). The attitude factors have been given names which reflect those original variables that are most highly correlated with them. This correlation of an original attitude question (variable) with a factor is called a loading. The first factor 'Social Interaction Patterns' is a measure of the social interaction and involvement between residents in a neighborhood. Factor two 'Local Territorial Identification' measures whether a resident indentifies more closely with the larger Des Moines metropolitan area (cosmopolitan) than with his local neighborhood territory. The third factor 'Degree of Isolation' measures the degree of isolation felt by a household toward life in general and toward the neighborhood in specific. These two facets are highly correlated (HRB, 1969).

Together these oblique factors are taken to be representative of the entire matrix of attitudinal responses since they explain such a high proportion of the total variance.

TABLE 1

RESIDENTIAL SATISFACTION ATTITUDE FACTORS AND FACTOR LOADINGS

Factor Number	Percent of Explanation of Total Variation Among the Original Variables	Loading[1]	Attitude Factor Name and Variable Names
1	27		SOCIAL INTERACTION PATTERNS (Seashore's Group Cohesiveness Scale)
		-0.652	Do you feel you are really a part of your area?
		-0.433	If you had a chance to do the same kind of work, for the same pay, in another area within Des Moines, how would you feel about moving from the area in which you now live?
		-0.781	The way in which members of the area get along with each other.
		-0.822	The way in which members of the area stick together.
		-0.804	The way that the members of the area help each other in their daily lives.
2	21		LOCAL TERRITORIAL IDENTIFICATION (Glazer's Cosmopolitan-Local Scale)
		0.377	It is more important to have people accept differences than it is to have community agreement.
		0.628	Time pressures make it awfully difficult for community members to have close personal contacts with one another, even though they would like to.

37

TABLE 1 (cont'd.)

Factor Number	Percent of Explanation of Total Variation Among the Original Variables	Loading[1]	Attitude Factor Name and Variable Names
		0.580	Considering other responsibilities, there is altogether too much demand on community members to participate in community activities.
		0.551	It is unfortunate but true that there are very few people around here with whom one can share his interests.
		0.459	One important way in which people are kept in line around here is through gossip.
		0.542	Even though they are competent and conscientious, somehow or another one gets very little stimulation from his neighbors in this community area.
		0.532	There are too many divisive cliques and groups in this community.
		-0.737	In our modern world, knowledge must be practical to be meaningful.
		-0.362	One of the nice things about this community is that the relationships are almost wholly cooperative and friendly.
		-0.635	It is desirable to have a community gathering. This would create a greater degree of agreement among us.

TABLE 1 (cont'd.)

Factor Number	Percent of Explanation of Total Variation Among the Original Variables	Loading[1]	Attitude Factor Name and Variable Names
3	18		**DEGREE OF ISOLATION** (Srole's Anomia Scale)
		0.748	It's hardly fair to bring a child into the world with the way things look for the future.
		0.737	In spite of what some people say, the lot of the average man is getting worse, not better.
		0.726	Nowadays, a person has to live pretty much for today and let tomorrow take care of itself.
		0.727	These days a person doesn't really know who he can count on.

[1] Source: Computed by the author
Only loadings greater than 0.35 are included;
for details see Harmon (1969)

The factor analysis also reduced the redundancies in-
herent in the 19 original questions and transforms this information into more useful data called 'factor scores'.

Table 2 summarizes the factor-analytically derived basic
dimensions for each of the 14 metropolitan sub-areas. See
map 1. The numerical entries in the table are mean area factor
scores on the dimensions. A high score on 'Social Interaction
Patterns' indicates a cohesive community characterized by a substantial degree of social interaction between residents in an
area; a low score indicates lack of social interaction. The
highest scores are outside of Des Moines, in the contiguous
suburbs of West Des Moines (4.528), Windsor Heights-Clive
(4.565). With the exception of the two areas in the central
city (3.239) and (3.462) the other area scores are close to the
metropolitan score (4.019). The central city areas have a
higher crime rate and a relatively transient population, neither
of which are conducive to resident interaction.

A high score on 'Local Territorial Identification'
indicates a strong local orientation, while a low score indicates that the respondents identify more closely with a larger
community. The Western and Central sections of Des Moines
have the lowest scores (3.587) and (3.420) respectively and
thus tend to be more cosmopolitan minded than the total Metro
area (4.074). Drake University is located on the Westside.
The area is thus characterized to a large extent by a transient

40

population whose overriding concern is with 'academia' and not with neighborhood affairs. The Park Avenue area is, for the

TABLE 2

MEAN AREA FACTOR SCORES
THREE RESIDENTIAL SATISFACTION ATTITUDE FACTORS

Name of area	Social Interaction Patterns	Local Territorial Identification	Degree of Isolation
Central	3.462	3.448	3.475
Model Cities	3.239	3.420	3.401
Highland Park	4.030	3.732	3.935
Northeast	4.151	3.727	3.675
East University	3.914	4.009	3.435
Park Avenue	4.204	3.705	4.019
Indianola Road	3.915	4.134	3.598
Drake University	3.744	3.587	4.185
Grand Avenue	4.205	4.207	4.543
Merle Hay	4.103	4.091	4.412
Beaverdale	4.336	4.599	4.079
Urbandale	3.929	4.208	4.453
Windsor Heights-Clive	4.565	4.638	4.258
West Des Moines	4.528	4.245	4.414
Metropolitan Des Moines	4.019	4.074	4.056

Source: Computed by author

most part, an older and comparatively affluent **area** with a

substantial number of professionals more likely to identify with

their professional or larger spheres of reference than with a

small geographical area. The two central sections are at the

other extreme of the socio-economic spectrum. They are poor

and the population, which includes the majority of the city's

Blacks, are very likely more concerned with finding and keeping jobs than with local affairs. The highest scores are found in the northwest (4.599) and in the suburbs (4.638). Both areas are newly developing, relatively affluent and the population is made up of young families who very likely find their area and local spatial identification quite important.

A high score on 'Degree of Isolation' indicates an area with a high degree of security and limited feelings of isolation by the households toward the area while a low score indicates the opposite. The metropolitan average is 4.056. The highest scores are found in the suburbs (4.453) and the westside (4.543). These areas have low crime rates, well-lighted streets and are considered relatively high-status areas. The low scores of the central (3.401) and eastside (3.435) areas indicate the level of apprehension felt by the residents of these low income sections which are characterized by more substandard housing, vacant buildings and relatively poorer street lighting.

These scores were mapped to show the spatial distribution of the three dimensions of residential satisfaction (see Figures 3 to 5). The results are revealing (especially Figure 5, Degree of Isolation). Metropolitan Des Moines is composed of three well defined spatial territories. At one extreme are the two central sections. They consistently rate low on all three dimensions. The remainder of the City of Des Moines can be divided into an

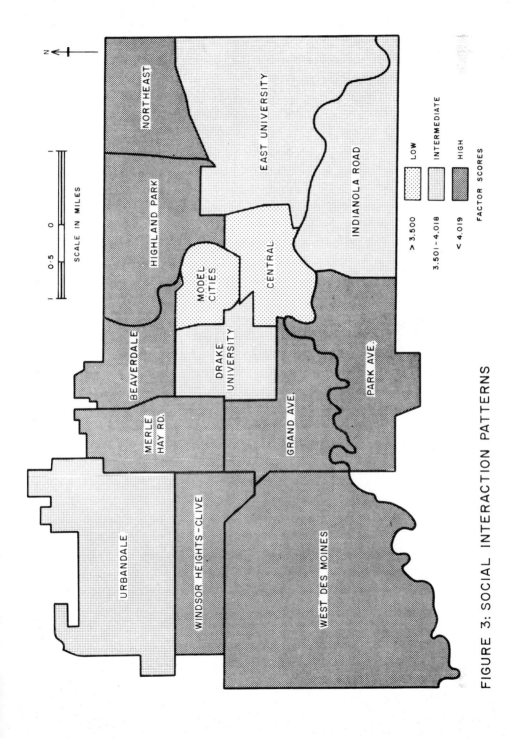

FIGURE 3: SOCIAL INTERACTION PATTERNS

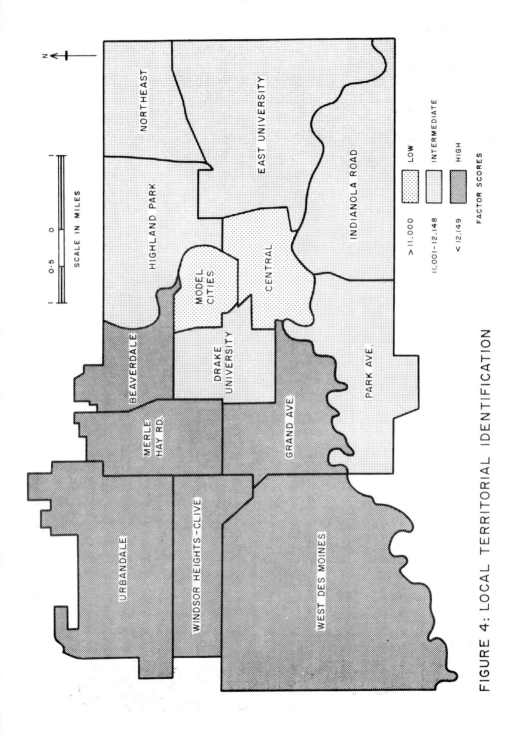

FIGURE 4: LOCAL TERRITORIAL IDENTIFICATION

SCALE IN MILES

FACTOR SCORES

LOW > 11.000

INTERMEDIATE 11.001-12.148

HIGH < 12.149

URBANDALE

WINDSOR HEIGHTS - CLIVE

WEST DES MOINES

BEAVERDALE

MERLE HAY RD.

GRAND AVE.

PARK AVE.

HIGHLAND PARK

MODEL CITIES

DRAKE UNIVERSITY

CENTRAL

NORTHEAST

EAST UNIVERSITY

INDIANOLA ROAD

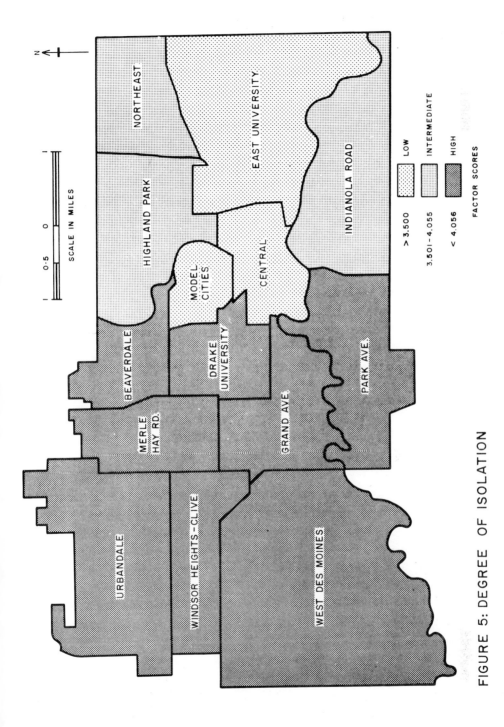

FIGURE 5: DEGREE OF ISOLATION

NORTHEAST

HIGHLAND PARK

EAST UNIVERSITY

MODEL CITIES

CENTRAL

INDIANOLA ROAD

BEAVERDALE

DRAKE UNIVERSITY

MERLE HAY RD.

GRAND AVE.

PARK AVE.

URBANDALE

WINDSOR HEIGHTS-CLIVE

WEST DES MOINES

N

SCALE IN MILES

0.5   0   I

LOW

INTERMEDIATE

HIGH

FACTOR SCORES

> 3.500

3.501 - 4.055

< 4.056

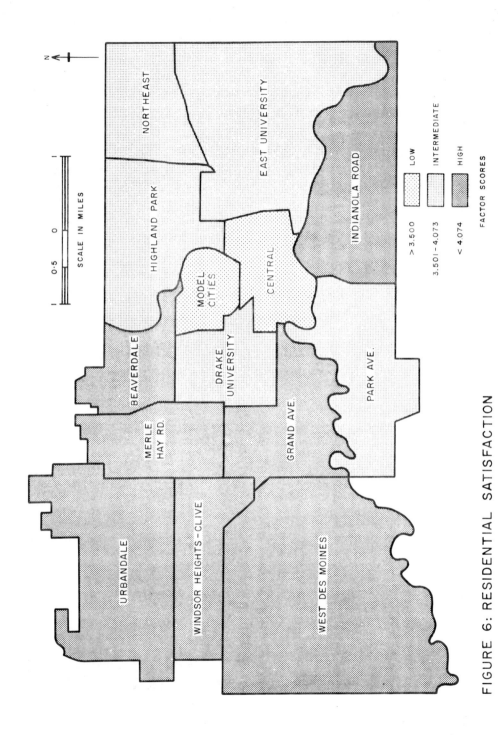

FIGURE 6: RESIDENTIAL SATISFACTION

46

eastern half and a western half. The western half is similar to the suburbs in terms of scoring on the dimensions of residential satisfaction. The eastern half ranks consistently next to the central sections. The three contiguous western suburbs consistently rate high on all three dimensions and form the other extreme.

These three factors define the basic dimensions within the substantive domain of 'residential satisfaction'. This research, however, is interested in the delineated functional interrelationships among the 19 varied phenomena mainly as empirical concepts to interrelate in a global description of a domain, in line with the discussion in the previous section. Consequently, to derive this more general and abstract 'higher

TABLE 3

FACTOR CORRELATION MATRIX

Social Interaction Patterns	Local Territorial Identification	Degree of Isolation	
1.00			Social Interaction Patterns
0.42	1.00		Local Territorial Identification
0.38	0.41	1.00	Degree of Isolation

Source: Computed by author

order' concept, the factor scores of the three basic and complementary dimensions were weighted according to their contribution to explanation and then additively combined into a
composite measure of residential satisfaction[1] (see Figure 6).

---

[1]This is defensible on the grounds that the factor correlations are small (see Table 3).

CHAPTER III

ESTIMATION OF PREFERENCES FOR HOUSING
ENVIRONMENT ATTRIBUTES

The second and third stages of the research strategy, to
be presented in this chapter, obtain the inter-subject similarities, aggregate the individual households into homogeneous
perceptual groups, and empirically estimate the preferences for
urban environmental attitudes. An evaluation function models
the differential saliences of attributes by estimating the
evaluative weights used by the household groups in making overall
ratings of their multi-attribute residential environment.

Aggregation of Households into Homogeneous
Perceptual Groups

Each individual household has his own level and quality
of experience with regard to the residential housing environment
and from this may emerge a unique set of aspiration and satisfaction levels. This research, however, is concerned with the
identification and documentation of generalizable differences
among household groups because these differences lead to insights
about basic processes of residential satisfaction behavior.
Study of individuals are necessary in this context because, as
Robinson (1950) has demonstrated associations between variables
which are established at the group level do not necessarily apply

49

to the individual level. On the other hand, individual studies can be validly generalized to groups and eventually to a population (Harrison and Sarre, 1971, p. 351).

The problem may be concisely stated in this way: How may the heterogeneous individual households that comprise the Des Moines metropolitan area sample be grouped into relatively homogeneous groups. This is essentially a question of numerical taxonomy (Grigg, 1969). But, behavioral science theories and accumulated empirical research findings provide guidelines and hypotheses for a behaviorist segmentation. They permit the identification of a relevant 'scale' at which determinants of residential satisfaction are operative (Sonquist, 1971). This requires research into relationships between 'Residential Satisfaction' and the household's demographic characteristics, socio-economic status and locationally-based perceptions to establish whether they can be used to predict differences in the first. In turn, such research feeds back incremental knowledge about the residential satisfaction process. The evaluative criterion to judge the quality of the aggregation strategy and search for predictors of generalizable differences in residential satisfaction behavior among household groups, reduces to operational questions of predictive efficacy (Johnston, 1968). There are an almost infinite number of ways in which households may be aggregated into homogeneous groups. The most frequently used bases are family-life-cycle stage, social class and geographic location.

Family-Life-Cycle

The concept of family-life-cycle as a major determinant of residential satisfaction is intuitively appealing. Therefore, to answer the critical question whether membership in different demographic segments leads to differential responses in residential satisfaction the Lansing and Kish (1957) schema of family-life-cycle (FLC) was applied in a multiple regression procedure with dummy variables to the total sample of 778 households.[1] The demographic characteristics of age, number, and age of children and marital status each were portioned into several categories. For example, age of respondent was divided into six categories, 24 years old and under, 25-34, 35-44, 45-54, 55-64 and 65 years of age and over. The number of persons in the household was divided into three categories: one person, two persons, three or more persons. Since the relationship of these persons to the head of the household was known the age of the children was categorized into two classes: under six years of age, and over. Marital status by definition is already a dichotomous variable.

---

[1] For the use of Dummy Variables in Regression Equations see Suits (1957).

51

Next a series of dummy variables were created -- one for each combination of the aforementioned categories. A given household's score takes on a value of one for one of the variables and zero for all others. The full set of variables were not included for estimation purposes because of high multicollinearity and an aggregation size constraint of at least 30 households per groups. Eight groupings were finally selected (see Table 4).

TABLE 4

FAMILY-LIFE-CYCLES[1]

Group Number	Brief Demographic Description
1	Young singles, under 24 years of age
2	Young married, No children
3	Young married, Young Child or Children, under six years of age
4	Married, Children over six years of age
5	Older Married, Children
6	Older Married, No Children
7	Older Single
8	Others

[1]Concept and definitions are based on Lansing and Kish (1957).

The resulting model looks like this:

$$RSA_j = \alpha + B_1 X_1 + \sum_{j=2}^{8} B_j X_{ji} + \varepsilon_i$$

where:

RSA_i residential satisfaction response of household i

α the intercept

$X_1, \ldots, X_8$ are the eight dummy variables

E_i is the error term

52

Notice that this formulation amounts to a multidimensional classification system in which the variables themselves represent the eight household groups.

Since the FLC classification explained only 3.5% of the variance and the resultant household groups were exceedingly heterogeneous in terms of their perceptions, which, in turn, led to residential satisfaction models with low predictive efficacy, it was not used to classify households. The FLC index was, however, retained as an explanatory variable.

Socio-Economic-Status

Through the use of dummy variables in a regression framework a respondent's classification based on such socio-economic variables as occupation, education, amount of income and home purchase price (Haer, 1957; Warner, 1949), revealed only a modest degree of association between 'social class' and residential satisfaction. While this casts doubt on the relative merits of 'social class' measures they were retained as an explanatory summary index.

There are a number of reasons that may account for the inadequacy of 'social class' measures to explain and predict a household's residential satisfaction. A single-dimensional view of social class does not appear to describe the complexities of determinants of human behavior. This is especially so because of recent social and economic development which tend to diminish differences in attitudes and behavior of supposedly different social classes (Coleman, 1960). A plausible explanation is advanced by sociologists, including Adams (1953), with the concept of status consistency or socio-economic congruence. In essence, this concept maintains that those with incongruent socio-economic positions, e.g. high education but not high income, and low occupation status, will tend to behave differently than those with congruent positions. The specific pattern of the inconsistency, e.g. low income and high education or high income and low education, may also affect behavior patterns.

However, no attempt is made here to pursue this line of reasoning any further. Wind (1969), cited in Frank et. al. (1972, p. 49), albeit in the context of consumer buying behavior, examined the relationship between social class measures and the degree of status consistency and found that neither were important explanatory variables; although the latter provided some improved insights to better understand behavior.

Common Perceptions of Residential Environments

What is the value of developing a multidimensional classification of the households based on the independent variables? The use of such a classification as a basis for predicting residential satisfaction assumes the existence of high-order interactions or non-linearities in the relationship between the dependent and in-

dependent variables. That is, the combined effects of some or all

of the housing environment perceptions would be considerably

greater than the sum of the individual effects. Because of a

lack of knowledge as to which high-order interactions exist,

households with similar profiles of scores over the measured chara-

cteristics will be grouped together.[1] This also reduces the

possibility of obtaining spurious results by diminishing the

influence of confounding and unmeasured variables (Blalock, 1964;

Sonquist, 1971).

A concise rationale for expecting that households in a

given environment have similar perceptual viewpoints is given by

Anderson (1962; p. 168).

> The principal spatial effect of the complicated pattern of
> personal and group preferences and hostilities can be
> presented, therefore, as a force pulling similar people
> together and driving dissimilar and hostile people and
> groups apart...The result is a partial, but relatively
> stable, separation of the major subgroups that comprise
> the city. Each group tends to live in its own neighborhood.

This contention is supported by Dobriner's study which identifies

basic differences in the behavior patterns of city families and

suburban families of the same general class, ethnic and religious

---

[1]On the average the intercorrelations between the raw
perception measures range around 0.15.

background which stem from sociological-ecological patterns including the physical characteristics of the communities (Dobriner,
1963, 1970; see also Boskoff, 1970).

Consequently, the hypothesis that the households in 14
sub-areas are characterized by relatively homogeneous perceptual
viewpoints was tested through a Multiple Discriminant Analysis.
The general objective of discriminatory analysis is to find a
linear combination of the housing environment perceptions to
discriminate maximally between predefined sub-areas while simultaneously minimizing variations within groups. In other words,
the discriminant function identifies dimensions of a classification just as principal components analysis identifies dimensions
of variability. The linear function associates in a classification,
the discriminant space, any household, any group center of
gravity, and the center of gravity of all households (Cassetti,
1968).

Table 5 shows the final F-matrix of the discriminant
analysis for each of the areal household groups. By comparing
the matrix entries and the computed F-statistic with appropriate
degrees of freedom, the statistical significance of the groups was
tested.

Overall, with three exceptions the household groups are
meaningful and characterized by relative homogeneous perceptual
viewpoints. There are, however, great variations in their

TABLE 5

DISCRIMINANT ANALYSIS[1] OF 13 PERCEPTUAL VARIABLES[2]
ALL 14 HOUSEHOLD GROUPS
F-MATRIX[3]

Group Acronym

Group Acronym[4]	CENTRAL	MODCIT	HIPARK	NOREST	EASTUN	PARKAV	INDIAN	DRAKEU	GRANDA	MERLEH	BEAVER	URBAND	WESTDM
MODCIT	42.71												
HIPARK	6.58	56.95											
NOREST	7.06	55.25	3.59										
EASTUN	4.59	46.98	3.87	5.54									
PARKAV	4.84	36.30	6.10	4.04	4.84								
INDIAN	5.64	47.73	6.59	5.05	4.41	4.23							
DRAKEU	6.28	60.40	2.44	4.52	2.95	3.78	6.19						
GRANDA	9.34	47.75	8.36	6.80	6.81	3.99	5.29	5.43					
MERLEH	8.50	65.06	3.61	5.12	5.00	4.27	6.80	2.85	5.92				
BEAVER	5.58	35.67	3.92	5.17	4.54	3.13	4.99	2.31	4.16	3.64			
URBAND	14.85	71.15	15.21	13.52	13.68	5.63	8.68	15.31	7.80	10.75	8.88		
WESTDM	11.16	59.38	15.73	13.95	11.25	5.30	5.98	13.48	6.23	12.26	7.95	6.44	
WHCLIV	11.69	52.01	10.75	8.54	9.60	4.23	6.63	9.08	5.18	8.13	7.90	6.85	8.62

[1] Analysis of Variance for the overall discriminant analysis, approximate F=10.43.

[2] For a list of these variables see Table

[3] Degrees of freedom for the F-Matrix (9,756), approximate F=1.93.

[4] For a definition see Table 6

Source: Computed by the author

distinctiveness. The Model Cities group and those of the three contiguous suburbs are most clearly and consistently distinct from each other and the city groups. The household groups located in the City of Des Moines, while statistically significant, are characterized by less homogeneity or distinctiveness of perceptual viewpoints. The least 'homogeneous' household group is Drake University most probably because it is largely composed of a transient and student population. The other two exceptions, because of small sample size, resulted in the aggregation of the suburbs of Windsor Heights and Clive, and in the allocation of the 10 residents of the Southeast sub-areas to Central. In the latter case all residents were clustered in the census tract adjacent to the Central area.

The whole aggregation scheme of grouping households into areal groups was tested and verified through a special feature of discriminatory analysis. It permits computation of probabilities of misclassification of individual households, using the squared distance from the group means of the 13 perceptual variables as a computational measure (Cassetti, 1968). For each of the 778 households probabilities of belonging to any of the 14 areal groups were calculated. Households were then allocated to a group according to the largest probabilities. Not including the Drake area the largest number of misclassifications in an area was 16% of the households, although for most

sections this figure ranged from 10 - 15% and a low of 2% (i.e.
one household) for the Model Cities. This degree of 'homogeneity'
was considered satisfactory since later analyses focus on the
heterogeneity of the 'homogeneous' groups. Table 6 lists the
final household groups by name and shows the number of households
which compose them. The smallest group is 'Park Avenue' with 30
households, the largest is 'Drake University' with 106 households.

TABLE 6

HOUSEHOLD GROUP NAMES, ACRONYM AND NUMBER OF HOUSEHOLDS

Group Names[1]	Group Acronym	Number of Households
Central	CENTRAL	39
Model Cities	MODCIT	44
Highland Park	HIPARK	74
Northeast	NOREST	50
East University	EASTUN	48
Park Avenue	PARKAV	30
Indianola Road	INDIAN	41
Drake University	DRAKEU	106
Grand Avenue	GRANDA	40
Merle Hay	MERLEH	81
Beaverdale	BEAVER	38
Urbandale	URBAND	75
West Des Moines	WESTDM	74
Windsor Heights-Clive	WHCLIV	38
Metropolitan Des Moines Total		778

[1]For locational reference see Figure 1.

The Variable Relationships to be Modeled

The basic research premise is that the satisfaction of a household with the housing it chose and is currently occupying, as reflected in responses to questions toward the multi-attribute dwelling-unit and residential environment, can be employed to make statements about housing preferences. A household's satisfaction with a given urban residential environment is affected not only by the attributes of the dwelling-unit but, it is also affected by accessibility to essential facilities and amenities, by symbolic values such as status and prestige of, and sense of identity with the environment as well as socio-economic characteristics of the household.

To model significant structural relationships between the variables of the residential satisfaction and preference model presupposes a knowledge of the relevant variables. These can be categorized into, at least, two groupings: (1) a household's perceptions of specific building and residential factors and (2) the socio-economic characteristics of the household. In this chapter the concern is only with the first group of variables. The other variables will be included in the analyses of inter- and intra-group differences in the next chapter.

Urban Environmental Factors

Of the myriad of possible urban environmental factors
only that subset of variables which the literature considers as
potentially 'relevant' contributors to residential satisfaction
were included.[1] These include accessibility to shopping, recreational and educational facilities, the provision of municipal
services such as public transportation, power and water supply
and garbage collection, physical attributes of the housing
structure as well as characteristics that measure appearance and
status of a residential environment, such as quiet streets and
natural features. This inquiry utilizes space as a relevant
variable because consideration of spatial factors, it is felt,
adds to a more complex explanation of urban residential satisfaction than is possible with only non-spatial variables.
Table 7 lists the 22 perceived social, physical, spatial and
esthetic attributes of the housing environment that were initially included.

At the start of the analyses, the extent of activity
and collinearity were checked for each variable in order to
determine which, if any of these perceptions would have to be
deleted. Six variables were eliminated from the analysis because
their rates of activity were so modest that they precluded an

---

[1]For details see the literature review; especially the
article by Wilson (1962) and the HRB-Study (1969).

TABLE 7

LIST OF 22 PERCEIVED SOCIAL, PHYSICAL AND ESTHETIC
ATTRIBUTES OF THE URBAN ENVIRONMENT

Variable Number of Original Variables	Variable Name	Acronym of Logarithmically Transformed Variable used in Final Analysis
1	Accessibility to supermarket	ACC1
2	Accessibility to shopping center	ACC2
3	Accessibility to recreation	ACC3
4	Accessibility to elementary school	ACC4
5	Accessibility to employment	ACC5
6	Sewer service availability	LGSERVIC
7	Separation of pedestrians and vehicles	SEPARATE
8	Quiet streets	QUIET
9	Residential area separate from commercial and industrial nuisances	PRIVATE
10	Natural features: trees, scrubs, grassy areas	NATLFEAT
11	Public transportation	TRANSP
12	Yards well maintained and free from junk	YARDS
13	Street condition	STCONDIT
14	Garbage collection	LGSERVIC
15	Public water service	LGSERVIC
16	Power supply	LGSERVIC
17	Modern education available for every person in area	--
18	People of different races, sexes, and nationalities have full opportunity to take part in community life	--
19	Cultural opportunities available to the area	--
20	Availability of medical and health care in area	--
21	Capable local government concerned with community betterment	--
22	Opportunity for citizens participation	--

Source: Questionnaire Survey; see Appendix A for full description of variables

assessment of their effects. Four more variables, sewer services, garbage collection, public water service and power supply were combined into an index of 'Municipal Services' because of collinearity. The remaining twelve variables, identified by their acronyms in Table 7, were transformed into logarithms to make the variables linear.[1]

The Functional Form of the Model

The choice of an appropriate functional form of the residential satisfaction model is crucial to the outcome of the analyses. While the question of representing preference judgments is an important one theoretically, in practice a hierarchy of models can be fitted. Green and Rao's (1972) research compares multi-dimensional scaling algorithms and related techniques at the conceptual level, presents methodological results and substantive implications to see if more elaborate preference models are justified by significantly better fits to the data. Clearly, the simpler models should be used if they provide reasonable descriptions of the manifest data. Blalock (1965) argues that additive models seem to approximate reality well

[1] A substantive interpretation of the logarithm of the household's response to, for instance, 'Quiet Streets' (variable 8) is that the response is based on the respondent's perceptions of all types of quiet streets in the neighborhood--dead-end streets, residential two-way streets etc.--and hence represents an 'averaged' response. Similar rationales exist for the other variables.

in many cases, but that common sense considerations often suggest specific types of non-additive models as alternatives, because of known, or suspected, interaction effects among the variables. Consequently, because a high degree of searching for non-linearities and interactions was deemed necessary to reduce the possibility of obtaining spurious results, a multiplicative model was initially formulated and tested.

The general conceptualization of the problem, methodology and technique are suggested by the psychologist Helson's (1947) 'Adaptation Level Theory'. Applied to the non-experimental problem context of residential satisfaction the concern is with the manner in which a person integrates information about a stimulus object, the residential environment and makes a judgment regarding residential satisfaction with respect to a set of relevant attributes of the stimulus object. The relationships between the attributes involved in the judgmental process it is posited, is multiplicative.[1] The general model looks as follows:

$$RSA_i = P^k Q^l R^m \qquad \ldots\ldots (1)$$

where

RSA_i is the residential satisfaction attitude response
of household i to the attribute combination of the
neighborhood stimulus.

---

[1]Limited substantive support was recently, and independently, provided by Shinn's (1972) methodological paper.

P, Q and R indicate perceptions of attributes k, l and

m are exponents.

This model implies that the relationship between subjective

values of the information stimuli (attributes) and the residential

satisfaction responses is linear in logarithms, thus:

$$\log RSA_i = k \log P + l \log Q + m \log R \quad ....(2)$$

This is of advantage in the computation of the exponents, which

now can be estimated through standard regression analyses.

The dependent variable (RSA) is the empirically derived

measure of residential satisfaction with the chosen housing

environment. It reflects the household's state of knowledge and

beliefs about the neighborhood but does not include an evaluative

dimension (Ramsay and Case, 1970, p. 185). A step-wise Multiple

Regression model was employed in which the evaluative reaction

to the stimulus urban environment is a consequence of summing the

product of the evaluative reaction to a relevant environmental

property and the stimulus scale value of that property across all

relevant properties. Since the scale values of the stimulus on

the relevant properties are known, a multiple regression of the

stimulus evaluations on the property scale values will provide

estimates of the preferences for the attributes and of their

relevance (Ramsay and Case, 1970, p. 185). The evaluative

reactions to the environmental stimulus are represented by the

standardized regression coefficients. The relevancy of the

attributes can be ascertained by ranking them, according to the
size of the standardized regression coefficients, and by testing
the statistical significance of the latter. The vector model
of preference structures, as used in this analysis represents
a relatively uncomplicated modeling effort. As such it has its
limitations. It constrains each of the households within the
homogeneous perceptual groups to share the rotation, in percep-
tual-evluative space, of the archetypical household. In other
words, the simple vector model fits vectors in the rotated and
differentially stretched space of the average subject.[1] There
are advantages as well with this aggregate analysis in addition
to less analytical and computing time than disaggregate analysis.
It can be assumed that observed differences between individuals
in a group are due to random error. Thus, it is assumed, the
true preference function is the same for all members of the
group and the research task is to pool the individual estimates
and responses in order to get the best possible estimate of
the group function. An additional advantage of the propounded

_____

[1]However drastic such an assumption may appear to be,
Green and Rao (1972, p. 113) present evidence, albeit in a different context, to suggest that relatively little appears to be
gained, sometimes, by using a less restricted model, which permits
idiosyncratic rotation and differential axis stretching for each
individual, in terms of predictive efficacy.

aggregate methodology is that it permits analysis and correlation of individual or subgroup differences in preferences with other characteristics of the respondents.

The preference derived with the multiplicative residential satisfaction model were tested against those derived through an additive model. A linear compensatory model, in effect a sub-class of the multiplicative functional form, assumes that the overall evaluation of the multi-attribute environment is equal to an additive combination of the component attributes. The model thus assumes that the individual attributes are scaled such that the more of each, the better. This, naturally, still necessitates the estimation of the importance weights of the components. It was found that the multiplicative non-linear model explained only slightly more, generally around three per-cent, of the variance in the dependent variable. In addition, Spearman Rank Order correlation coefficients were computed for the urban environmental preferences. These range from 0.86 to 0.95 for the 14 household groups, indicating a high degree of consistency between the linear and the multiplicative residential satisfaction model.

Thus it would be tempting to conclude that the multipli-cative model 'reduces' to the simpler linear model and that a main-effects, additive combination is adequate to account for this evaluative context. A more plausible, and intuitively

appealing, explanation is that the model is still multiplicative
but that it is linear over the range of responses. At some
point, therefore, one could expect the law of diminishing re-
turns to set in.[1] The multiplicative model, therefore, is
considered to be superior to the additive model of residential
satisfaction and will be employed here.

<u>Residential Satisfaction as a Function of</u>
<u>Urban Environmental Preferences</u>

The quantitative assessment of current residential satisfaction permits the identification and measurement of preferences,
held by the fourteen homogeneous household groups, for attributes of
their housing environment.

Fourteen regression equations, one for each household group,
are presented in this section which summarize the findings, and
facilitate their interpretation (see Table 8). The dependent
variable is the empirically derived measure of overall residential
satisfaction with the chosen residential environment. The independent variables are the thirteen environmental attributes of
the environmental stimulus. The table shows the name of each
relevant variables its standardized regression coefficient, and
the associated F-value which measures the statistical significance of that independent variable's contribution to the

---

[1]Personal communication from Allen M. Shinn, Jr., July 5,
1972.

68

statistical explanation of the dependent variable. The standardized regression coefficient (beta) represents the 'evaluative' weighting of a particular attribute of the environment by a household group. The relevancy of the attributes can be ascertained by ranking them according to the magnitude of their betas, and by testing the statistical significance of the latter (as shown in Table 8); results of the analyses, including statistically insignificant variables, may be found in Appendix B.

A general check on the validity of the evaluative model, separately for each household group, is provided by the multiple correlation coefficients (R). These range from 0.41 to 0.89 for the complete equations, with most ranging upwards from 0.75. More specifically, the validity of the modeled relationships between residential satisfaction and urban environmental attributes was tested through an Analysis of Variance. Table 9 shows that all F-values are statistically significant at the 0.05 level. In substantive terms this means that the 'independent' urban environmental attributes substantially 'explain' the 'dependent' variable residential satisfaction.

In this analysis it was difficult to isolate the causes from the effects, since a household chose a residence based on his attitudes, but, conversely, the residential attitudes are molded by the residence he chose. The two interact and are jointly determined. This interaction between cause and effect

69

is manifested in the signs of the betas. A positive numerical entry in Table 8 means that as a household's residential satisfaction increases, it increasingly attaches importance to a specific residential characteristic; for instance accessibility to shopping center and maintenance of yards. A plausible interpretation is that the household has chosen a residential evironment which conforms to his preferences with regard to accessibility and maintenance of yards.

A negative numerical entry is more difficult to interpret. If residential satisfaction tends to increase as the distance to elementary school increases, we might interpret the respondents' preference for accessibility as a reflection of some irritation due to the absence of an elementary school at proximity. The preferences are not fulfilled, hence the negative beta weight. In the first case the degree of access might be viewed as the effect of the attitude, and in the second case, it might be viewed as the cause.

The summary table shows some important findings. Irrespective of group membership households evaluate and weight relatively few environmental attributes as relevant contributors to the explanation of residential satisfaction. On the average only between four and six variables are considered; exceptions are the Indianola and Drake household groups with three and nine variables respectively. It is, therefore, posited that a

TABLE 8

SUMMARY OF REGRESSION ANALYSES OF RESIDENTIAL SATISFACTION[1]
URBAN ENVIRONMENTAL PREFERENCES
FOR 14 HOUSEHOLD GROUPS

Variable Acronym	Beta	F - Value
CENTRAL (R = 0.78)		
QUIET	-0.786	24.547
YARDS	0.602	9.036
TRANSP	-0.526	20.498
SEPARATE	0.471	8.710
ST CONDIT	-0.337	5.558
MODEL CITIES (R = 0.67)		
YARDS	-0.574	15.687
NATLFEAT	0.211	2.788
ACC4	0.199	2.760
LGSERVIC	-0.178	2.600
NORTHEAST (R = 0.67)		
ACC1	-0.666	23.982
SEPARATE	-0.382	11.201
ACC2	0.367	7.762
TRANSP	0.283	5.761
ACC5	0.238	4.480
HIGHLAND PARK (R = 0.78)		
SEPARATE	-0.356	14.423
PRIVATE	-0.281	10.018
ACC4	-0.278	8.080
TRANSP	-0.247	6.687
YARDS	0.218	5.804
NATLFEAT	0.161	3.071
ACC1	0.136	2.803

TABLE 8 (cont'd)

Variable Acronym	Beta	F - Value
	EAST UNIVERSITY (R = 0.85)	
LGSERVIC	0.683	53.016
TRANSP	-0.447	25.952
YARDS	-0.434	20.606
ST CONDIT	-0.293	10.668
ACC2	0.276	10.631
QUIET	-0.203	5.023
	PARK (R = 0.77)	
ACC1	0.531	15.623
ST CONDIT	0.447	10.891
QUIET	-0.356	6.988
ACC4	-0.312	5.437
	INDIANOLA (R = 0.61)	
NATLFEAT	0.560	13.439
SEPARATE	-0.417	8.809
LGSERVIC	-0.385	6.603
	GRAND (R = 0.70)	
SEPARATE	0.512	16.359
ST. CONDIT	-0.353	7.756
QUIET	-0.310	5.857
NATLFEAT	0.282	4.922
ACC4	-0.244	3.798

TABLE 8 (cont'd)

Variable Acronym	Beta	F - Value
	DRAKE (R = 0.67)	
YARDS	-0.389	14.326
ACC1	0.381	21.159
ACC2	-0.363	17.958
QUIET	-0.263	7.170
LGSERVIC	0.242	3.641
PRIVATE	-0.240	4.882
TRANSP	0.195	3.690
ACC3	-0.189	5.897
ACC4	-0.158	3.873
	MERLE HAY (R = 0.34)	
ACC3	0.249	4.748
ACC2	-0.244	4.509
NATLFEAT	-0.173	2.528
	BEAVERDALE (R = 0.58)	
TRANSP	-0.419	6.634
ACC3	0.347	4.286
ACC4	-0.275	2.776
ACC2	0.235	2.651
	URBANDALE (R = 0.74)	
QUIET	-0.375	19.692
ACC4	-0.366	19.342
YARDS	-0.336	15.351
ACC5	-0.165	3.972

TABLE 8 (cont'd)

Variable Acronym	Beta	F - Value
WEST DES MOINES (R = 0.55)		
ST CONDIT	0.434	9.800
SEPARATE	-0.385	10.826
LGSERVIC	-0.296	4.516
ACC5	-0.283	7.106
PRIVATE	-0.218	3.939
WINDSOR - CLIVE (R = 0.79)		
PRIVATE	-0.507	15.206
YARDS	-0.429	14.177
ACC4	0.373	9.201
NATLFEAT	-0.339	8.028
ACC3	-0.338	7.296

[1]Only statistically significant variables are shown.
For complete regression analyses which include all variables see
Appendix B.

Source: Computed by author

TABLE 9

ANALYSIS OF VARIANCE FOR THE REGRESSION
ANALYSIS OF RESIDENTIAL SATISFACTION
FOR 14 HOUSEHOLD GROUPS[1]

Name of Household Group	Degrees of Freedom	Computed F-Value	Significant at the 0.05 Level
CENTRAL	5,33	10.025	YES
MODEL CITIES	4,39	7.759	YES
NORTHEAST	5,44	7.166	YES
HIGHLAND PARK	7,65	12.158	YES
EAST UNIVERSITY	6,41	17.146	YES
PARK AVENUE	4,25	7.987	YES
INDIANOLA ROAD	3,37	7.129	YES
GRAND AVENUE	5,34	6.486	YES
DRAKE	10,95	7.886	YES
MERLE HAY	3,77	3.288	YES
BEAVERDALE	4,33	3.690	YES
URBANDALE	4,70	21.149	YES
WEST DES MOINES	5,68	5.385	YES
WINDSOR - CLIVE	5,32	10.112	YES

[1]Only statistically significant variables are included in this regression analysis. For complete regression analyses which include all variables see Appendix B.

Source: Computed by author

person confronted with the residential judgment task can only organize and process between three and six attributes, and even then, probably, combines them in an additive fashion. Shepard (1964) provides experimental research evidence in psychology to support this finding, as does Wind (1968, p. 40) in marketing. Based on his empirical evidence the latter notes that as the number of attributes in the evaluative context increased no statistical attribute interactions were found, and the main effects model provided a good approximation of how respondents combine importance weights for individual attributes.

Many of the findings of the Regression Analyses are interesting and have logical explanations; for example, the overall importance of some accessibility considerations across most of the groups. Other findings are more difficult to interpret and rather than yielding evidence to support pre-conceived relationships, they uncover relationships which can form the basis of new hypotheses. Several of these associations such as those between public services and residential satisfaction, may be the result of inadequate sampling techniques or they may have arisen randomly. Intuitively, it seems unlikely that households would be overly concerned with such their residential environment. On the other hand, they may be valid though unanticipated and explainable only on tentative grounds, and require further analysis (see Daly, 1968, p. 46).

In order to better understand the spatial variability of the derived preferences a table was compiled which shows the frequencies
of occurrence of urban environmental preferences for household
groups (see Table 10). These groupings are identified by their
location as inner city, suburb and city, logically divisible into
distinctive east and west parts. While Figure 1 shows their
location, Figures 3 to 6 show the associated residential satisfaction measures.

Each of the variables listed in Table 10 could have become
a preference fourteen times, once for each group. This, however,
did not occur. Instead, only two preferences 'accessibility to
elementary school' and 'yards well maintained and free of junk'
are common to half or more of the groups. A study by Weiss
et. al. (1966), in which new home purchasers were asked which of
thirty-nine factors were important to them in choosing their
present home, and which would be in any future choice, found
similar results. The accessibility factors were relatively
unimportant in the present and future choices, and, of the
proximity measures, only nearness to schools proved significant.

The next most common preferences, shared by six groups
are 'separation of pedestrian and vehicles', 'quiet streets',
'natural features: trees, shrubs, grassy areas' and 'public
transportation'. Preferences for accessibility to work and

shopping were derived for only three of the fourteen household
groups. Although this is somewhat surprising it must be emphasized

TABLE 10

FREQUENCY OF OCCURRENCE OF URBAN ENVIRONMENTAL PREFERENCES
FOR HOUSEHOLD GROUPINGS

Variable Acronym	Total Metropolitan[1]	Central[2]	Suburbs[3]	City[4]	Eastern City[5]	Western City[6]
ACC1	4	–	–	4	2	2
ACC2	5	–	–	5	2	3
ACC3	4	–	1	3	–	3
ACC4	8	1	2	5	1	4
ACC5	3	–	2	1	1	–
LGSERVIC	5	1	1	3	2	1
SEPARATE	6	1	1	4	3	1
QUIET	6	1	1	4	1	3
PRIVATE	4	–	2	2	1	1
NATLFEAT	6	1	1	4	2	2
TRANSP	6	1	–	5	3	2
YARDS	7	2	2	3	2	1
STCONDIT	5	1	1	3	1	2

1   All fourteen household groups are included
2   Composed of Central and Model Cities groups
3   Urbandale, West Des Moines, Windsor-Clive
4   Includes the nine city groups with the exception of both
     central groups
5   Included are Northeast, Highland Park, East University and
     Indianola groups
6   Included are Park, Grand, Drake, Merle Hay and Beaverdale groups

that Des Moines is a relatively small metropolitan area which has

a good east-west and north-south freeway system. It is readily

accessible to most metropolitan residents but peripheral to

households in Urbandale, West Des Moines and the Northeast who,

consequently, consider accessibility to work important. In

contrast neither the Central nor the Eastern city groups reveal
a preference for accessibility to work. This appears to contra-
dict the economic rent theories (Alonzo, 1964) because in this
research it is generally those with higher incomes and occupational status who placed a premium on closeness to employment,
and esthetic environmental qualities. Research by Logan (1968)
would suggest that the relative insignificance of work place
location as an influence on residential satisfaction is because
of a breakdown of the metropolitan area into a number of relatively independent employment fields in addition to the central
business district. Stegman's(1969, p. 22) claim that accessibility appears to be an 'inferior good' for most households and
that suburban families consider residential quality and esthetics
as important as accessibility, is partially supported by the
findings presented in Tables 8 and 10.

Equally important to the frequency of occurrence of
urban environmental preferences is the absence of preferences for
certain attributes. For example, none of the three suburban
groups revealed any preferences for good public transportation,
no doubt because of the common use of private automobiles; whereas five out of the nine city groups expressed such preferences.
This contradicts the findings of the nationwide HRB (1969) study
which concluded that similar proportions of city and suburban
householders drive to work, invalidating the usual assumptions

that central city locations are preferred because cheap public transport can be used. A plausible reconciliation of these separately derived and conflicting findings may be that the Des Moines metropolitan area may not reflect the recent trends that Stegman and the HRB study indicate. In addition, it is probable that Stegman's conclusions are rather too sweeping in dismissing the role of access in residential location.

In conclusion, there are significant spatial variations and, paradoxically, at the same time there is much spatial order in the Des Moines metropolitan area in terms of urban environmental preferences. In addition, different levels of the urban residential housing environment are considered important by the archetypes representing the households in a given area. In the city, accessibility considerations and public transportation preferences are significant. This is in addition to preferences for such environmental factors as 'separation of pedestrians and vehicles' and 'quiet streets'. In the central city area, by contrast, preferences relate more specifically to improvements in the quality of the immediate housing environment. The suburbs are different again. There, residential considerations such as privacy and esthetic preferences as well as accessibility to work place are significant contributors of residential satisfaction.

CHAPTER IV

ANALYSIS OF INTRA AND INTER-GROUP DIFFERENCES

In the last chapter households were successfully aggregated into relatively homogeneous groups based on commonality of perceptions of residential attributes. This made it possible to derive ex post facto housing environment preferences for an archetypical individual of each group. It is the purpose of this chapter to analyze intra and inter-group differences. For instance, it is expected that there is a substantial degree of heterogeneity within the homogeneous perceptual-evaluative groups in terms of socio-economic-demographic characteristics and in terms of the effects of a few selected processes of inter-personal influence. The chapter will also develop inter-group differences in urban environmental preferences by comparing and contrasting the archetypes with a metropolitan norm.

The Influence of Household Characteristics

Sociological and social-psychological theories of stratification emphasize the dependence of one's behavior on his social environment. There exists a multitude of primary and secondary social groupings that define an individual's place in the social order and demand certain behaviors of him (Festinger et. al., 1950). In an effort to measure these relationships and their

effect on residential satisfaction this research will use a
multiple regression model. The ten variables that were initially
included are listed in Table 11. At the start of the analyses
the extent of activity and collinearity were checked for each
variable in order to determine if any of these socio-economic
demographic variables would have to be deleted. Only one variable
(Size of Former Residential Community) was eliminated because of
a modest rate of activity. The second last variable (Monthly
Rent) was highly collinear with variable seven (Type of Dwelling
Unit) and was therefore deleted from all subsequent analyses.
In the case of the remaining variables problems revolving around
the suspected existence of interaction effects, and, to some
extent, inter-correlations necessitate special attention and
analytic innovations to be described in the following sections.

Socio-Economic-Status

Social classes, according to Berelson and Steiner (1964),
are relatively permanent, substantial, homogeneous divisions in
society with similar values, interests, life-styles and behavior.
The literature in the field of social stratification contains no
consensus over the appropriateness of various concepts of stratification and the indicators which may be employed to represent
them (Warner et. al., 1949; Laumann, 1966).

TABLE 11

SOCIO-ECONOMIC-DEMOGRAPHIC VARIABLES USED IN THE
ANALYSES OF INTRA-GROUP DIFFERENCES

Variable Number	Variable Name
1	Race
2	Raw Age
3	Years of School Completed
4	Occupation
5	Income of Household
6	Number of Persons in Household
7	Type Dwelling-Unit
8	Length of Residency at Present Address
9	Size of Former Residential Community
10	Monthly Rent
11	Purchase Price of Home

Source: Questionnaire Survey; see Appendix A for details.

Haer (1957, p. 54) states:

Some students have tried to lessen this confusion through
studies of the logical and empirical foundations of the
indices of social stratification. One useful approach in-
volves the careful delineation of characteristics of
important indices. Another line of inquiry investigates
whether correlations exist among a variety of indices in
current use. A third approach . . . concerns the relationships between stratification indices and other phenomena.
Findings of this kind may help to provide a basis for
evaluating the relative utility of several indices in terms
of their efficacy in providing predictions and generalizations.

Assuming, with Haer, that there is no 'ultimate' index which awaits

discovery the question of the 'best' index of stratification can be pragmatically decided on the basis of scientific utility. The problem then becomes one of selecting from a variety of equally feasible concepts and indices one which is reliably related to and predictive of a phenomenon of particular interest. Haer's (1957, p. 544) empirical work shows that Warner's (1949) 'Index of Status Characteristics' (ISC) has the highest coefficients of relative predictability to attitudes indicating community satisfaction.

Haer suggests that the superiority and greater efficiency of the 'Index of Status Characteristics' over several other well-known indices is related to its distinguishing features. It is a composite index and thus incorporates information pertaining to several areas of stratification. Through assignment of weights and scale scores, for each respondents type of occupation, house type, dwelling area and amount and source of income, the ISC provides a continuous series of ranks which appears to be a more fruitful theoretical approach than dividing society into a relatively small number of discrete categories (Haer, 1957, p. 545-546). Haer's findings imply that the more useful concept of stratification should embody several components rather than reflect only one aspect of behavior, or attitude. However, Haer does not suggest which components are appropriate.

Since Haer's approach appears to offer the greatest scientific utility, a factor analysis of socio-economic variables

established the appropriate loadings, or weights, to combine occupation, education, amount of income and home purchase price into
a Socio-Economic-status (SES) index. Table 12 summarizes this
information.

TABLE 12

WEIGHTS FOR COMPONENT VARIABLES OF
SOCIO-ECONOMIC-STATUS INDEX[1]

Status Characteristics	Factor Loading	Weight
Occupation	0.501	5
Education	-0.200	-2
Amount of Income	-0.744	-7
Home Purchase Price	0.614	6

[1]Components are similar to those in Warner's (1949) index.
Source: Computed by author.

The negative weights can reasonably be interpreted as
corrections for over-weighting. For example, income alone is
not significantly related to SES and participation. It is so
related only when that income is reflected in house purchase
and probably other symbols of social-class participation (Warner,
et. al., 1949, p. 178). For each individual household a numerical value of the logarithmically transformed socio-economic-
status index was thus derived.

One of the basic concerns of this analysis is the differential effects of various social environments on residential

satisfaction. But, the way in which a particular environmental factor influences residential satisfaction may depend on other environmental factors, on other characteristics of the individual, or on both. Thus, to represent the relationships between such a set of explanatory factors adequately may require interaction terms. Sonquist (1971, p. 50) illustrates the correspondence between substantive theoretical propositions which indicate differential environmental effects and the analytic concept of statistical interaction. According to Sonquist (1971, p. 44) at least three elements exist in a 'contextual conditional relationship' aimed at assessing the impact of the properties of group structure on the behavior of individuals. These are the notion of a relationship between two variables; the assumption that behavior varies with the environment or is somehow affected by it; and finally, the notion of differential effects of the environment on behavior -- that individuals of one kind may be affected differently by one environment than those of another kind.

The following reasoning and methodology are aimed at the specific task of assessing the impact of neighborhood socio-economic conditions on the relationship between conceptually similar variables defined on an individual level. Differential environmental effects are, clearly, not confined to small face-to-face informal groups or formal organizations. The characteristics

of a neighborhood may also influence residential satisfaction
(Sonquist, 1971, p. 48).

If individuals within a neighborhood strive for acceptance
by the dominant group and therefore bias their social contacts
in that direction, the pressures toward similarity of residential
satisfaction attitudes will be accentuated. In other words, it
is posited here that the effects of the socio-economic status of
the local environment serves as an important means of residential
orientation for a person, regardless of whether or not he shares
the social status of his neighbors. Indeed, it may be especially
so if the individuals socio-economic status is well above or well
below the residential area's average (see Segal and Meyer, 1971).
An answer is also sought to the question of whether or not the
environment's socio-economic status effect is greater than the
individual's own socio-economic status as a predictor of
residential satisfaction.

Methodologically, each area was described by the mean score
on the index of socio-economic status (SES) of respondents living
in it. The population sample was then statistically divided
into thirds through the use of dummy variables. Where an individual's SES was well above the area's average the new variable
was given the acronym NEWSES2. Where an individual's SES was well
below the area's average the new variable was given the acronym
NEWSES1. The relationships between 'individual' variables were

then examined separately for the new groups (see Tannenbaum and Bachman, 1964).

Family-Life-Cycle

The concept of family-life-cycle, generally an index of some or all of the demographic characteristics of sex, age, marital status, number and age of children, as a determinant of residential satisfaction is intuitively appealing. The logic underlying the use of a composite measure of family-life-cycle is that interactions occur between the component variables. Lansing and Kish (1957, p. 513) write that it is well known that changes occur in people's attitudes and behavior as they grow older, but many of these changes are associated less with 'age' per se than with influence of age upon an individual's family membership.

The critical dates in the life-cycle are when a change occurs in family status, such as marriage, the birth of a child, etc. Therefore, they rightly emphasize that, to understand an individual's social behavior, it is more relevant to consider which stage in the life-cycle he has reached rather than how old he is. Lansing and Kish (1957) propose 9 stages in the family-life-cycle and provide empirical evidence that the concept is theoretically more plausible and its performance is superior to 'age' as a variable. In an effort to assess the

influence of stage in the family-life-cycle on residential satisfaction this concept will be used on an explanatory variable.
Since the concept was developed and referred to earlier in this
research, no further details are given here (see Table 4).

Length of Residency

Recent research has shown that additive modeling of time
related facets of the socialization process does not provide
good initial approximations of reality (Gulick, Bowerman and
Black, 1962; Sonquist, 1971, p. 51). Variables which are
intuitively considered explanatory of residential satisfaction,
such as an individual's age and length of residency at the current
address, i.e. exposure to a particular environment, involve time
and may be involved in interaction terms. An individual early in
the stages of the socialization process may react differently to
attributes of the residential stimulus than one with longer
residency and, hence, familiarity of the attitudes, beliefs and
behavior of the neighborhood group. The research by both Golledge
(1969) and Horton and Reynolds (1969) develops this point in some
detail.

An analysis of the relationship between length of residency
and residential satisfaction, it is thus posited, necessitates to
account for the conditional dependence, or interaction effect of
the former and age of the respondent at the time of the interview.

This is so because age is an important proxy variable for a number of significant social processes. Consequently, the variable 'age' was categorized into three classes: individuals who are under 30 years, between 31-54 years, and 55 years old and over. Again, through the use of dummy variables 'length of residency' was simultaneously considered. It was categorized into length of residency at the current address: 'one year or less', 'between one and five years', and 'five years and over'. This resulted in nine categories which are identified in the summary table by the acronym LOGSATIS.

Additional Household Characteristics

Two additional individual correlates of residential satisfaction were systematically investigated. In an attempt to test whether home ownership or rental status and race are important predictors of residential satisfaction, two further dummy variables (1,0) were created. The two classes of the first variable, identified in the summary table by the acronym NEWTYPE, indicate ownership of a single family dwelling-unit and renters of an apartment or duplex respectively. The second variable, given the acronym NEWRACE, categorizes white and non-white population respectively. As Suits (1957) points out linearity and normality assumptions need not be made, although additivity is, of course, assumed.

Residential Satisfaction as a Function of Urban Environmental Preferences and Household Characteristics

The last chapter demonstrated that urban environmental preferences are good and valid predictors of residential satisfaction. Nevertheless, the addition of household characteristics to the modeled relationships, which may be considered as beloning to a different level in the developmental sequence, substantially increased the amount of explanation.[1] The increase ranges from a low of seven percent for the Urbandale group to a high of twenty-five percent for the Merle Hay group. For most household groups it ranges around twelve to fifteen percent of the variance in residential satisfaction. In six groups over 80% of the variance is explained. Merle Hay and West Des Moines are the only groups in which less than 50% of the variance is accounted for. This finding indicates a poor fit of the model and a lack of knowledge about additional variables.

To facilitate interpretation of the regression equations which model the functional relationships between residential satisfaction and urban environmental preferences and household

---

[1]Hyman (1955, p. 256) writes that: 'an explanatory factor that is psychological and a control factor that is sociological can be conceived as two different levels of description, i.e. one might regard an attitude as a derivative of objective position or status or an objective position in society as leading to psychological processes, such as attitude. Thus, the concept of spuriousness would not be appropriate.'

characteristics for the 14 household groups, summary Table 13 is
included. The table shows that urban environmental preferences
are still the most important predictors of residential satisfaction; indicated by the size of the betas. The only exception
occurs in the Park, Grand and Merle Hay household groups.

Of the seven household characteristics included in this
analysis only two, length of residency and the individual's
socio-economic status, are of importance to more than a single
household group. Table 13 shows that length of residency,
conditionally dependent on the age of the respondent, is, as
was expected, a significant predictor of residential satisfaction
in seven household groups; Northeast, Indianola, Grand, Drake,
Merle Hay, Beaverdale, Urbandale. In each case the relationship
is positive. This suggests that as the length of exposure to
the residential housing environment and, no doubt, personal
contact within it increases, residential satisfaction increases
also. This effect is especially pronounced as the age of
the individual increases.

The socio-economic status of the individual household is a
significant predictor of residential satisfaction in four household groups; Northeast, Highland Park, Park, Drake. In each
of these cases there is a negative relationship, suggesting
that as individual's socio-economic status increases there is a

TABLE 13

SUMMARY OF REGRESSION ANALYSES OF RESIDENTIAL SATISFACTION
URBAN ENVIRONMENTAL PREFERENCES AND HOUSEHOLD CHARACTERISTICS
FOR 14 HOUSEHOLD GROUPS[1]

Variable Acronym	Beta	F-Value
CENTRAL (R = 0.95)		
QUIET	-1.336	35.966
YARDS	0.923	15.759
LGSERVIC	0.759	10.026
TRANSP	-0.710	10.186
ACC2	-0.574	11.620
NEWTYPE	-0.542	7.394
NATLFEAT	-0.506	12.229
PRIVATE	0.391	3.668
STCONDIT	-0.316	3.639
MODEL CITIES (R = 0.79)		
YARDS	-0.455	6.653
NATLFEAT	0.349	4.282
LOGFLC	0.310	4.359
ACC4	0.246	3.286
NORTHEAST (R = 0.84)		
ACC1	-0.602	18.658
NEWSES2	0.480	5.137
LOGSATIS	0.457	11.352
LOGSES	-0.364	1.262
ACC2	0.359	7.216
SEPARATE	-0.295	4.305
HIGHLAND PARK (R = 0.83)		
SEPARATE	-0.363	10.522
LOGSES	-0.345	2.420
NEWSES2	0.338	2.766
ACC4	-0.305	7.554
PRIVATE	-0.289	8.473
NEWRACE	-0.268	5.654
YARDS	0.245	5.047

93

TABLE 13 (cont'd)

Variable Acronym	Beta	F-Value
TRANSP	-0.214	3.261
ACC1	0.199	3.612
NATLFEAT	0.191	4.127

EAST UNIVERSITY (R = 0.90)		
LGSERVIC	0.815	27.053
TRANSP	-0.618	19.206
STCONDIT	-0.347	7.688
YARDS	-0.339	6.092
ACC2	0.249	4.288

PARK (R = 0.91)		
LOGSES	-0.722	2.321
PRIVATE	0.529	3.768
NEWSES1	-0.497	2.158
QUIET	-0.495	7.825
ACC5	0.469	6.060

INDIANOLA (R = 0.78)		
NATLFEAT	0.634	14.559
YARDS	-0.455	4.607
SEPARATE	-0.398	6.558
LOGSATIS	0.288	2.960

GRAND (R = 0.89)		
LOGSATIS	0.505	8.639
ACC5	0.449	6.270
SEPARATE	0.428	6.000
QUIET	-0.334	2.705

DRAKE (R = 0.76)		
QUIET	-0.337	12.797
ACC1	0.325	13.774
STCONDIT	0.321	8.999

TABLE 13 (cont'd)

Variable Acronym	Beta	F-Value
YARDS	-0.317	8.296
ACC2	-0.282	9.251
LOGSATIS	0.267	7.644
LOGSES	-0.249	4.963
ACC3	-0.224	8.234
PRIVATE	-0.200	3.387

MERLE HAY (R = 0.62)

LOGSATIS	0.357	8.605
ACC2	-0.257	5.306
ACC1	-0.252	5.360
ACC3	0.248	4.927
ACC5	0.231	4.117
NEWTYPE	0.171	2.709

BEAVERDALE (R = 0.85)

TRANSP	-0.772	11.705
LGSERVIC	0.467	2.854
ACC3	0.455	7.534
LOGSATIS	0.384	5.092

URBANDALE (R = 0.82)

QUIET	-0.356	9.743
ACC4	-0.306	8.833
LOGSATIS	0.234	4.475
ACC2	0.187	2.816
ACC3	-0.184	3.252

WEST DES MOINES (R = 0.66)

STCONDIT	0.471	10.600
SEPARATE	-0.461	10.616
LOGSES	0.372	5.638
ACC5	-0.337	8.231
PRIVATE	-0.288	4.840

TABLE 13 (cont'd)

Variable Acronym	Beta	F-Value
WINDSOR - CLIVE (R = 0.91)		
YARDS	-0.421	4.255
ACC4	0.331	3.771

[1] Only statistically significant variables are shown. For complete regression analyses which include all variables see Appendix C.

Source: Computed by the author.

concomitant reduction in his residential satisfaction. A possible explanation of this finding for the Drake group appears
to be that individuals of higher socio-economic status find the
transient academic population and associated lack of residential
territorial identification and, possibly, maintenance and absence
of strong social interaction patterns (see Table 2) detrimental
to their own residential satisfaction. Similar arguments can be
advanced for the Northeast and Highland Park groups. Illucidation of the puzzling nature of this finding as it applies to the
Park group, essentially an older and affluent area, is sought
by relating the individual's socio-economic status to the
area's socio-economic status. Unfortunately, only the relationship between individual's whose socio-economic status
places them in the lowest third of the area's socio-economic
status (NEWSES1) and residential satisfaction is significant.

This relationship is negative, suggesting that individuals of substantially lower socio-economic status then most of their neighbors find their residential, and possibly social aspirations thwarted which reflects on their residential satisfaction. By consulting the results of the complete regression analysis in Appendix C, it was found that NEWSES2 is positively related to residential satisfaction. The direction of this relationship is intuitively plausible and self-explanatory. In the Northeast and Highland Park groups it can similarly be argued, based on the significant positive relationship between NEWSES2 and residential satisfaction as presented in Table 13, that those individuals are cognizant of the facts of their socio-economic eminence relative to most of their neighbors and this contributes to their residential satisfaction.

Interestingly enough, racial considerations are not a significant predictor of residential satisfaction in the Central and Model Cities groups, where most of the city's non-white, black, population lives. Instead, it is an important predictor for the Highland Park group, located contiguous to both central city sections. There is a significant negative relationship between white population and residential satisfaction which has been related, in other research, to the presence of blacks (see Ermuth, 1972). It must be noted that census tracks two and three, which form part of the areal extent of the Highland

Park household group (see Figure 7) have black populations in excess of five percent.

The relationship between homeownership and residential satisfaction was significant for only the Central and Merle Hay groups. The fact that the relationship is negative for the former is, no doubt, related to the fact that the area is characterized by more substandard housing and vacant buildings than all other parts of the metropolitan area. For the Merle Hay group the relationship is positive, suggesting that homeowners are more satisfied than renters of apartments or duplexes. It must be noted that virtually all of the households in the other areas live in and own single family dwelling units. This may explain why the dichotomous variable is not a good predictor of residential satisfaction.

Unanticipated, and rather disappointing, is the fact that the concept of family-life-cycle (LOGFLC), as operationalized here, was a significant predictor for only one household group, Model Cities. There, LOGFLC has a positive relationship with residential satisfaction, suggesting that as an individual's stage in the life-cycle advances there is an increasing degree of residential satisfaction.

Inter-Group Differences

In order to assess the potential influence of the conditions in a local environment upon the perception and evluation of urban environmental attributes as contributors to residential satisfaction, a Covariance Analysis is conducted. The hypotheses to be tested were whether the general residential conditions differ in the areas or whether the respective households perceive and evaluate their urban environment differently. In other words, is there homogeneity in the functional relationships between the dependent variable, residential satisfaction, and the independent variables for the separate samples. No technical description of Covariance Analysis will be presented here (for details see Kneipp et. al., 1967). In Covariance Analysis a difference in general residential conditions exists if the slopes of the regression lines are parallel but the intercepts differ. If the intercepts are the same but the slope of the regression lines are different than households perceive and functionally integrate, the urban environmental attributes differently.

The results of the analysis confirmed essential homogeneity of regression.[1] It is thus statistically reasonable to consider

---

[1] This was achieved after Bartlett's test for homogeneity of variance had proven that the dependent variable is homoscedastic among the 14 household groups.

the subgroup regression lines as being from the same population, except for variations in the origin (Kneipp et. al., 1967, p. 5). The quantitative variables, therefore, are subject to the same functional relationships within the groups.[1]

Derivation of Metropolitan Evaluative Dimensions

The last section demonstrated that all household groups derive their urban environmental preferences by essentially the same process of integration and evaluation of attributes of the stimulus object. It is the purpose of the remainder of this chapter to demonstrate the differences that exist between the archetypical individuals which represent the household groups. Because of the particular data base this necessitates methodological innovation.[2] Consequently, a metropolitan norm is derived to serve as a standard for comparison between the household archetypes.

Methodologically this is achieved by deriving major urban environmental preference dimensions for the metropolitan Des Moines population sample as a whole. By relating each of the

_____

[1]The results of the analysis also confirmed that the areal membership of households is statistically significant and increases the explanatory power of the regression model, albeit minimally.

[2]Each household was asked, in the interview survey, to relate all his responses to only his own local residential area.

household archetype urban environmental preference vectors to this norm their inter-group differences are revealed. More specifically, a data matrix is formed in which the 14 archetypes form the observational entities and their respective 13 urban environmental preferences, the beta weights, form the variables. The variables are then grouped through an Oblique Factor Analysis. In this way, it is possible to derive four distinct metropolitan dimensions of urban environmental preferences. These dimensions are named after the original preferences that are most highly correlated with them (see Table 14). In order of importance they are Neighborhood Environment, Housing Environment, Shopping Accessibility and Employment and Transportation. The findings emphasize that the current residential satisfaction of a 'typical' metropolitan Des Moines resident is primarily based on the Residential Environment, relating to the quality of services, quiet streets and their condition, the separation of pedestrians and vehicles and the existing natural features. Secondarily, it is based on the Housing Environment, relating to yard maintenance and privacy, proximity of the house to an elementary school, quiet streets and proximity of the house to a recreational facility. To a lesser extent it is based on Shopping Accessibility, to a supermarket and to a shopping center. Lastly, it is based on Employment and Transportation preferences, relating to accessibility to work and availability of public

TABLE 14

METROPOLITAN DES MOINES
DIMENSIONS OF URBAN ENVIRONMENTAL PREFERENCES
MATRIX OF FACTOR LOADINGS[1]

Variable Acronym[2]	Factor 1 Neighborhood Environment	Factor 2 Housing Environment	Factor 3 Shopping Accessibility	Factor 4 Employment and Transportation
ACC1	-0.00180	-0.09605	-0.99750	-0.25293
ACC2	-0.22106	0.22368	0.40907	0.05792
ACC3	-0.08706	-0.56628	-0.13386	-0.05637
ACC4	-0.16116	0.75060	0.27015	-0.10647
ACC5	0.08277	-0.05672	0.18374	0.64817
SEPARATE	0.60383	-0.13889	-0.20357	-0.03853
QUIET	-0.74383	0.56155	0.30626	-0.12218
PRIVATE	0.14937	-0.65686	-0.01205	0.58505
NATLFEAT	-0.47209	0.15626	-0.03820	0.34272
TRANSP	-0.55101	0.24590	0.27293	0.58882
YARDS	0.31804	-0.82365	-0.15179	-0.05472
STCONDIT	-0.72825	-0.07529	-0.13518	-0.13726
LGSERVIC	0.91939	-0.18309	-0.19266	-0.20481
EIGENVALUES	3.872	2.310	1.863	1.119
CUMULATIVE PROPORTION OF TOTAL VARIANCE	0.298	0.476	0.619	0.719

[1]Only loadings greater than 0.35 were used to name the dimensions. These are underlined. For computational reasons see Harmon (1969).

[2]For variable definitions see Table 7.

Source: Computed by the author.

transportation.

These four dimensions together explain about 72% of the variance of the original thirteen urban environmental preferences. This is considered highly satisfactory. In addition, the dimensions are collinear only to a nominal extent (see Table 15). This means that they are, indeed, distinct and virtually independent, or orthogonal, which is necessary for the inter-group comparison.

TABLE 15

METROPOLITAN DES MOINES
DIMENSIONS OF URBAN ENVIRONMENTAL PREFERENCES
OBLIQUE FACTOR ANALYSIS: FACTOR CORRELATIONS

	Factor 1	Factor 2	Factor 3	Factor 4
FACTOR 1	1.000	-0.192	-0.104	-0.068
FACTOR 2	-0.192	1.000	0.199	-0.031
FACTOR 3	-0.104	0.199	1.000	0.138
FACTOR 4	-0.068	-0.031	0.138	1.000

Source: Computed by the author.

Relationship Between Household Archetypes and
Metropolitan Des Moines Norms

In an effort to demonstrate inter-group differences in urban environmental preference an innovative use of a multiple regression model was necessary to relate each household archetype separately to the metropolitan Des Moines norms.

More specifically, each archetype preference vector, consisting of the thirteen beta weights, was regressed against the
loadings of the four metropolitan dimensions of urban environmental preferences (see Table 14). The resulting regression
coefficients were standardized. They now represent estimates of
how the archetype's urban environmental preference dimensions are
related to the metropolitan dimensions. In effect, they measure
the extent of over or under- evaluation in a given evironment
due to variations in general residential conditions (see Table
16). Again, the validity of the modeled relationships is presented by the coefficient of determination, the squared
coefficient of multiple correlation (R) (shows in Table 16).
For eleven of the fourteen archetypes the model is highly
significant. The three exceptions are Highland Park, Urbandale,
and Merle Hay for which none of the beta weights are significant.
An example, or two, will help to make clear the substantive meaning
of the beta weights. A typical household in the Central section overevaluates 'neighborhood environment' preferences relative to the metropolitan norm due to the relatively low desirability of these residential factors (for comparison see Table 8,
Urban Environmental Preferences). The 'housing environment',
on the other hand, is underevaluated relative to the metropolitan
norm due to a predominant concern with residential factors and

a general satisfaction with the existing housing environment.
This contrasts sharply with a typical household in the Model
Cities area whose primary concern is with the housing environment. Another example will suffice to demonstrate the inter-
group differences summarized in this table. A typical household in the Northeast area expresses strong preferences for
'shopping accessibility' because no large shopping centers are
near. We should, therefore, expect that a typical household
in the Beaverdale area which is near two large shopping centers,
does not exhibit such preferences.

Indeed, as Table 15 shows, 'shopping accessibility' is
the least important preference dimension of that archetype,
relative to the metropolitan norm.

TABLE 16

RESULTS OF REGRESSION ANALYSES OF THE
RELATIONS BETWEEN A HOUSEHOLD GROUP AND METROPOLITAN DES MOINES
IN TERMS OF DIMENSIONS OF URBAN ENVIRONMENTAL
PREFERENCES

Factor Name	Beta	F-Value
CENTRAL (R = 0.96)		
Neighborhood Environment	0.532	22.577
Housing Environment	-0.449	11.132
Shopping Accessibility	-0.176	1.160
Employment and Transportation	0.091	0.181
MODEL CITIES (R = 0.71)		
Housing Environment	0.715	5.734
Shopping Accessibility	-0.382	2.383
Employment and Transportation	0.288	0.941
Neighborhood Environment	-0.161	0.291
NORTHEAST (R = 0.90)		
Shopping Accessibility	0.745	16.980
Employment and Transportation	0.302	3.325
Housing Environment	-0.292	2.537
Neighborhood Environment	-0.193	1.343
HIGHLAND PARK (R = 0.39)		
Shopping Accessibility	-0.284	0.461
Neighborhood Environment	-0.191	0.247
Housing Environment	-0.167	0.156
Employment and Transportation	-0.134	0.123
EAST UNIVERSITY (R = 0.80)		
Neighborhood Environment	0.814	10.521
Housing Environment	0.529	3.669
Employment and Transportation	-0.211	0.719
Shopping Accessibility	-0.044	0.026

TABLE 16 (cont'd)

Factor Name	Beta	F-Value
PARK AVENUE (R = 0.89)		
Neighborhood Environment	-0.715	14.926
Housing Environment	-0.544	7.126
Shopping Accessibility	-0.495	6.033
Employment and Transportation	0.447	5.897
INDIANOLA ROAD (R = 0.79)		
Neighborhood Environment	-0.763	9.160
Shopping Accessibility	-0.507	3.420
Employment and Transportation	0.303	1.432
Housing Environment	0.085	0.094
GRAND AVENUE (R = 0.58)		
Neighborhood Environment	0.574	3.834
Employment and Transportation	0.317	1.873
Shopping Accessibility	-0.173	0.217
Housing Environment	0.144	0.147
DRAKE (R = 0.74)		
Shopping Accessibility	-0.934	9.303
Housing Environment	0.576	3.452
Employment and Transportation	0.391	1.960
Neighborhood Environment	0.051	0.033
MERLE HAY (R = 0.46)		
Housing Environment	-0.548	2.305
Shopping Accessibility	0.259	0.609
Neighborhood Environment	-0.223	0.416
Employment and Transportation	-0.033	0.031

TABLE 16 (cont'd)

Factor Name	Beta	F-Value
BEAVERDALE (R = 0.88)		
Employment and Transportation	-0.843	18.871
Housing Environment	-0.618	8.271
Neighborhood Environment	-0.255	1.771
Shopping Accessibility	0.071	0.111
URBANDALE (R = 0.39)		
Shopping Accessibility	-0.334	0.636
Employment and Transportation	0.086	0.047
Neighborhood Environment	-0.185	0.233
Housing Environment	-0.197	0.216
WEST DES MOINES (R = 0.96)		
Neighborhood Environment	-1.035	80.319
Employment and Transportation	-0.413	12.987
Housing Environment	-0.209	2.698
Shopping Accessibility	-0.049	0.127
WINDSOR - CLIVE (R = 0.87)		
Housing Environment	0.871	19.400
Neighborhood Environment	0.148	1.508
Shopping Accessibility	0.113	0.249
Employment and Transportation	-0.082	0.157

Source: Computed by the author.

CHAPTER V

SUMMARY AND CONCLUSIONS

Given a belief that there is spatial order to residential patterns and processes within a metropolitan area this research illucidates current urban residential satisfaction as a modeling function of environmental preferences and household characteristics.

The wider research problem is founded on the premise that individual households operate in their urban environment based on decisions about the perceived environment and not as it exists in objective, physical terms. To achieve an adequate degree of explanation of urban residential satisfaction, therefore, necessitates the difficult task of incorporation of the perceived environment into the conceptual and the empirical methodology. This research suggests a number of ways to solve this problem.

The basic substantive assumption underlying the preference methodology employed here is that people react to environmental stimuli on the basis of their internalized organization of events, their 'perceptual map', and that a variety of judgmental phenomena can be related to how perceptual maps are used. Preference judgments, therefore, can be meaningfully represented as transformations of the respondent's perceptual map (Green and

Rao, 1972; Rushton, 1969).

This research incorporated the perceptions of urban households of attributes of their current residential environment. It
identifies elements of the environment upon which households
place a positive value and the absence of which is perceived as a
disutility. It also estimates the relative importance of these
values, and of the variations in their relative importance as
functions of variations in the characteristics of the individuals
and, to a lesser extent, variations of attributes of the environment. Because of this research is based on ex post facto housing
choice behavior, and, hence, current residential satisfaction or
dissatisfaction, it does not attempt to solve the most difficult
part of the wider research problem. To do this would involve the
development of rules which would link the preferences to choice
situation. The research does, however, develop a standard of
comparison of alternative residential environments.

The fact that this research deals with current residential
satisfaction poses another limitation. It does not permit discrimination between three types of urban environmental
preferences that may be related to residential satisfaction
(see Horton and Reynolds, 1969; Pred, 1967). These may be
ordered in terms of a 'threshold preference' representing the
lowest level of acceptability, an 'action preference' representing

the level or goal of residential achievement that is sought, and an 'ideal preference'. In the interview survey these three may or may not, have been combined by the respondents. At any rate, since it is not possible to separate them there is a need for conservatism in interpreting the responses which contain the latent preferences. All derived urban environmental preferences are, therefore, considered to be at least, the threshold preference level.

Some of the substantive and methodological contributions of this research may be summarized as follows:

(1) Urban residential satisfaction was meaningfully operationalized, after a rigorous theoretical discussion, in terms of three basic dimensions. These dimensions relating to a household's social interaction patterns, local territorial identification and degree of isolation are assumed to be representative of overall residential satisfaction. It reflects the household's state of knowledge and beliefs about the environment but does not include an evaluative dimension. This is crucial to the methodology which, in evaluative attribute space, derives the preferences for specific factors of the housing and residential environment.

(2) Residential areas vary by location within the metropolitan urban area. Associated with this is a variability in the spatial distribution of the three dimensions of residential satisfaction

that divides Des Moines into three well defined territories. The central city sections, at the lower end of the extreme, are characterized by low degrees of local territorial identification and social interaction and by a strong feeling of isolation by the households toward the area. The suburbs are at the other extreme. They are characterized by limited feelings of isolation, a strong local orientation and by a substantial degree of social interaction between residents in an area. The remaining city areas can be divided into an eastern half and a western half. The western half is similar to the suburbs in terms of scoring on the dimensions of residential satisfaction. The eastern half ranks consistently next to the central sections. (3) To find the appropriate subgroup configurations at which the determinants of residential satisfaction are operative, and to deal with the suspected existence of high-order interactions and non-linearities in the variable relationships, households are aggregated on the basis of commonality of perception of attributes of the residential environment. This led to the identification of fourteen distinct and relatively homogeneous perceptual points of view in the study areas. Family-life-cycle and socio-economic characteristics, although intuitively appealing, were found to be unsatisfactory aggregation criteria. (4) To replicate the process by which a person integrates information about the stimulus object and makes judgments regarding residential satisfaction with respect to a set of relevant attributes of the urban environment a model, originally developed in psycho-physics, was applied to this non-experimental context. It thus became possible to derive preferences that are latent in the household's perception responses. The relationship between the environmental attributes involved in the judgmental process was found to be multiplicative, as expected.

(5)   All household groups derive their urban environmental preferences by, essentially, the same process of integration and evaluation of attributes of the residential stimulus object. A general check on the validity of the evaluation-function model, separately for each household group, is provided by the multiple correlation coefficients. These range from 0.41 to 0.89 for the complete equations with most ranging upwards from 0.75. In substantive terms this means that the 'independent' urban environmental attributes substantially 'explain' the 'dependent' variable residential satisfaction.

(6)   Irrespective of group membership households evaluate and weigh relatively few environmental attributes as relevant contributors to residential satisfaction. In general, only between four and six variables are considered. Based on this empirical evidence it is concluded that a person confronted with the resi-

dential judgment task can only effectively organize and process these few factors in the evaluative context.

(7)   Preferences for accessibility to shopping and recreational facilities and place of work were relatively unimportant. Only nearness to elementary schools proved significant to half or more of the household groups.

(8)   In contradiction to economic rent theory principles, it was found, however, that higher income and occupational groups tend to have strong accessibility to place of employment preferences.

(9)   The urban environmental preferences that are common to half or more of the fourteen household groups are 'yards well maintained and free of junk', 'separation of pedestrians and vehicles', 'quiet streets', 'natural features' and 'public transportation'.

(10)   Equally important to the frequencies of occurrence of urban environmental preferences is the absence of preferences for certain attributes. For example, none of the three suburban groups revealed any preferences for public transportation, no doubt because of the common use of private automobiles; whereas five out of nine city groups expressed such preferences. Although this is somewhat surprising and contradicts the findings of the nationwide Highway Research Board (1969) study, which concluded that similar proportions of city and suburban house-

holders drive to work, it must be emphasized that Des Moines is a relatively small metropolitan area which has a good and balanced transportation system.

(11)   There are significant spatial variations and, paradoxically, at the same time there is much spatial order in the Des Moines metropolitan area in terms of urban environmental preferences. In addition, different levels of the urban environment (dwelling-unit, residential environment, metropolitan services) are pre-ferred depending on the location of a household group. In the city accessibility considerations, public transportation, and such environmental factors as 'separation of pedestrians and vehicles' and 'quiet streets' are preferred. In the central city areas, by contrast, preferences relate more specifically to improvements in the quality of the immediate housing environ-ment. In the suburbs residential considerations such as privacy and esthetic preferences as well as accessibility to work are significant contributors to residential satisfaction.

(12)   The addition of socio-economic and demographic house-hold characteristics, which may be considered as belonging to a different level in the developmental sequence, to the modeled functional relationships between residential satisfaction and urban environmental preferences substantially increased the amount of 'explanation'. The increases range from a low of seven

percent to a high of twenty-five percent but most are around twelve to fifteen percent of the variance of residential satisfaction. Interestingly, of the seven characteristics included in the analyses only two, length of residency and the individual's socio-economic status, are of importance to more than a single household group.

(13) Length of residency at the current address, conditionally dependent on age of the respondent is a significant predictor of residential satisfaction in seven household groups. This suggests that as the length of exposure to the urban environment increases so does residential satisfaction. This effect is especially pronounced as the age of the respondent increases.

(14) Racial considerations are negatively related to residential satisfaction. It is of interest to note that this characteristic does not have an important influence in the Central and Model Cities groups, where most of the city's non-white, black, population lives. Instead, it is of importance in the Highland Park group which is contiguous to the central area and has a non-white population in excess of five percent, but less than fifteen percent.

(15) The contextual effects of the residential environment's socio-economic status on the residential satisfaction of individuals whose own socio-economic status is well above or well below the environment's average was significant in only three household groups. This suggests that environmental socio-economic

status does not serve as an important means of residential orientation for many individuals.

In a specific way, the findings fulfill the stated research objectives; in a more general way, they raise more questions than they provide answers. There is the difficult problem of the temporal stability of the identified urban environmental preferences (see Rushton, 1969). There are the already mentioned limitations in the interpretation of the preferences since they are functionally related to current residential satisfaction. Other research questions relate to the congruency between the derived preferences and those estimated on the basis of hypothetical contexts. There are aggregation problems relating to the grouping of households into homogeneous perceptual classes and the associated loss of detail (see Green and Rao, 1972; Ruchston, 1969). In the long-run these research problems need detailed attention. However, this research increases our understanding of consumer preferences for attributes of spatially distributed housing environments through improvements in the identification of indicators of the relationship between a household and his urban environment. The research assumes that responses of a household expressing current satisfaction with environmental factors are more reliable indicators of housing preferences than hypothetically phrased preference questions often posed to those without knowledge and experience of the alternatives. It thus establishes the relative priorities of spatial, physical and social attributes as they contribute to residential satisfaction. In past research, partially because of limited data bases and partially because of concern with hypothetical situations, this was not possible. While the findings are not directly applicable elsewhere, the statistical reliability of the data, the fact that Des Moines is not undergoing any dynamic changes in population growth and composition, and the methodology make the generalizations and this research of general interest to other metropolitan areas of similar size and composition.

BIBLIOGRAPHY

Adams, S. Status Congruency as a Variable in Small Group
Performance, Social Forces. Vol. 32 (1953), pp. 16-22.

Alonzo, William. Location and Land Use. Cambridge: The MIT
Press, 1964.

Anderson, Theodore. Social and Economic Factors Affecting the
Location of Residential Neighborhoods, Papers, Regional
Science Association, Vol. 9, 1962, pp. 168-174.

Ardrey, Robert. The Territorial Imperative. New York: Dell
Publishing Company, 1966.

Atkisson, A.A., and Robinson, Ira. Amenity Resources for Urban
Living, H. S. Perloff (ed), The Quality of the Urban
Environment. Baltimore, Resources for the Future Inc.
1969, pp. 179-204.

Bell, Wendell. Social Choice, Life Styles, and Suburban
Residence, in William M. Dobriner (ed). The Suburban
Community. New York: Putnam, 1958.

Berelson, B. and Steiner, G. A. Human Behavior: An Inventory
of Scientific Findings. New York: Harcourt, 1964.

Beshers, James. Urban Social Structure. New York: The Free
Press, 1962.

Blalock, Hubert M. Jr. Causal Inferences in Non-Experimental
Research. Chapel Hill: The University of North Carolina
Press, 1964.

_____ Theory Building and the Concept of Interaction, American Sociological Review, Vol. 30, 1965,
pp. 374-380.

Bordessa, Ronald. Perception Research in Geography: An Appraisal
and Contribution to Urban Perception, Seminar Papers, No.
8. Newcastle, England: Department of Geography, University
of Newcastle, 1969.

Boskoff, Alvin. The Sociology of Urban Regions. New York:
Appleton, Century-Crofts, 1970.

Boyce, R. R. Residential Mobility and Its Implications for Urban
Spatial Change, Proceedings, Association of American
Geographers, Vol. 1, 1969, pp. 22-26.

Brookfield, H.C.   On the Environment as Perceived, in C. Board et. al. (eds). Progress in Geography, London: Arnold 1969.

Brown, L. and Moore, Eric.   The Intra-Urban Migration Process: A Perspective, Geografiska Annaler, Series B., Vol. 52B, No. 1, 1970.

Carr, Stephen and Schissler, Dale.   The City as a Trip, Environment and Behavior. Vol. 1, No. 1, 1969, pp. 7-35.

Cassetti, E.   Multiple Discriminant Functions. Research Report, No. 11, Evanston, Illinois: Northwestern University, 1968.

Cattell, R. B.   Factor Analysis. New York: Harper, 1952.

Central Iowa Regional Planning Commission. Community Analysis, Housing Report No.1, Des Moines, Iowa, July 1971.

Christaller, Walter. Die Zentralen Orte in Sueddeutschland. Jena: Fischer Verlag, 1933.

Clark, T.N.   Community Structure and Decision Making: Comparative Analyses. San Francisco: Chandler Publishing, 1968.

Coombs, C.H.   A Theory of Data. New York: Wiley and Sons, 1967.

Curtis, R. F. and Jackson, Elton.   Multiple Indicators in Survey Research, American Journal of Sociology, September 1962, pp. 195-204.

Daly, M.T.   Residential Location Decisions, Australian and New Zealand Journal of Sociology, Vol. 5, 1968, pp. 18-35.

Dawes, R. M.   Social Selection Based on Multidimensional Criteria, Journal of Abnormal and Social Psychology, Vol. 68, January 1964 1964, pp. 104-109.

Denham, C.   Attitudes Toward the Environment, Discussion Paper, No. 18. London: London School of Economics, Graduate School of Geography, 1968.

Deutsch, Karl W.   The Nerves of Government. New York: The Free Press, 1966.

Dobriner, W. M. Class in Suburbia. Englewood Cliffs: Prentice-Hall, 1963.

_____ The Growth and Structure of Metropolitan Areas, in Robert Gutman and D. Popenoe, (eds). Neighborhood, City and Metropolis. New York: Random House, 1970.

Doherty, J. M. Residential Preferences for Urban Environments in the United States, Discussion Paper, No. 29. London, England: Graduate School of Geography, London School of Economics, 1968.

Edwards, A. L. Techniques of Attitude Scale Construction. New York: Appleton Century-Crofts, 1957.

Elmar, Frank L., and Sutherland, Duncan P. Urban Design and Environmental Structuring, Journal, American Institute of Planners, Vol. 27, No. 1, pp. 38-41.

Ermuth, Frederick. Intra-Urban Space Preferences for Grocery Shopping, Pre-Conference Papers, Canadian Association of Geographers, 1970, pp. 117-123.

_____ Revealed Urban Residential Satisfaction. A Report presented to the Central Iowa Regional Planning Commission, Des Moines, Iowa. Iowa City, Iowa: Institute of Urban and Regional Research, University of Iowa, March 1, 1972.

Fendrich, J.M. A Study of the Association Among Verbal Attitudes, Commitment and Overt Behavior in Different Experimental Situations. Social Forces, 45, 1967, pp. 347-355.

Festinger, Leon et al. Social Pressures in Informal Groups. New York: Harper, 1950.

Fishbein, Martin (ed). Attitude Theory and Measurement. New York: Wiley and Sons, 1967.

Frank, R. E. et al. Market Segmentation. Englewood Cliffs: Prentice-Hall, 1972.

Fried, Marc and Gleicher, P. Some Sources of Residential Satisfaction in an Urban Slum, Journal, American Institute of Planners, Vol. 27, No. 4 (November), 1961, pp. 305-315.

_____ Functions of the Working-Class Community in Modern Urban Society, Journal, American Institute of Planners, Vol. 27, No. 2, 1961. pp. 90-101.

Gans, H. T. Urban Villagers. New York: The Free Press, 1962.

_____ Planning For People, Not Buildings, Environment and Planning, Vol. 1, 1969, pp. 33-46.

Glaser, B. G. The Local - Cosmopolitan Scientist, American Journal of Sociology. Vol. 69, 1963, pp. 245-259.

Golledge, R. and Rushton, Gerard. Multidimensional Scaling: Review and Geographic Applications, paper prepared for a meeting of the International Geographical Union, Poznan, Poland, September 1970.

_____ The Geographical Relevance of Some Learning Theories in Kevin Cox and R. G. Golledge, (eds). Behavioral Problems in Geography. Evanston, Illinois: Northwestern University Press, 1969, pp. 101-146.

Gouldner, Alvin W. The Norm of Reciprocity, American Sociological Review, Vol. 25, 1957, pp. 161-178.

_____ Cosmopolitans and Locals: Toward an Analysis of Latent Social Roles, Administrative Science Quarterly, Vol. 2, 1956, pp. 281-306 and pp. 444-480.

Green, P. E. and Carmone, Frank. Multidimensional Scaling and Related Techniques. Boston: Allyn and Bacon, 1970.

_____ and Rao, Vithala. Applied Multidimensional Scaling, New York: Holt, Rinehart and Winston, 1972.

Greenbie, B. B. New House or New Neighborhood, Land Economics, Vol. 45, 1968, pp. 359-365.

Grigg, David. Regions, Models and Classes, in R. J. Chorley and P. Haggett, Models in Geography. London: Methuen, 1969, pp. 461-501.

Gulick, J., Bowerman, C.E. and Back, K.W. Newcomer Enculteration in the City, in Chapin, E. S. and Weiss, S.W. (eds), Urban Growth Dynamics. New York: Wiley, 1963.

Gutman, R. Site Planning and Social Behavior, in Kates, R. W. and Wohlwill, J. F. (eds.). Man's Responses to the Physical Environment. The Journal of Social Issues, Vol. 22, No. 4, October 1966, pp. 103-115.

Haer, John L. Predictive Utility of Five Indices of Social Stratification, American Sociological Review, Vol. 22, October 1957, pp. 541-546.

Hall, Edward T. The Hidden Dimension. New York: Doubleday, 1969.

Harmon, H. Modern Factor Analysis. Chicago: University of Chicago Press, 1969.

Harrison, J. and Sarre, P. Personal Construct Theory in the Measurement of Environmental Images, Environment and Behavior, December 1971, pp. 351-374.

Helson, Harry. Adaptation-Level as Frame of Reference for Prediction of Psychophysical Data, The American Journal of Psychology, Vol. 60, January 1947, pp. 1-29.

Heyman, Mark. Space and Behavior, Landscape. Vol. XIII, Spring, 1964, pp. 4-10.

Hillery, G. A. Communal Organization: A Study of Local Societies. Chicago: University of Chicago Press, 1968.

_____ Definitions of Community: Areas of Agreement, Rural Sociology, Vol. 20, p. 119, 1969.

Hoinville, G. Evaluating Community Preferences, Environment and Planning, Vol. 3, 1971, pp. 33-50.

Homans, G. The Human Group. New York: Harcourt, 1950.

Horton, F. E. and Reynolds, D.R. An Investigation of Individual
     Action Spaces, Proceedings, Association of American
     Geographers, Vol. 1, 1969, pp. 70-75.

Hyman, Herbert. Survey Design and Analysis. Glencoe, Illinois:
     The Free Press, 1955.

Johnston, R. J. Choice in Classification: The Subjectivity of
     Objective Methods, Annals of the Association of American
     Geographers, September 1968, pp. 575-589.

_____ Urban Residential Patterns. London: G. Bell
     and Sons, 1971.

Kain, J. F. and Quigley, J. M. Evaluating the Quality of the
     Residential Environment, Environment and Planning, Vol. 2,
     1970, pp. 23-32.

Kneipp, Stanley et al. GAC: A Computer Program for Analysis of
     Linear Covariance, Discussion Paper, No. 6. Iowa City, Iowa:
     Department of Geography, The University of Iowa, June 1967.

Lamanna, Richard A. Value Consensus Among Urban Residents,
     Journal, American Association of Planners, Vol. 30, No. 4
     November 1964, pp. 317-323.

Landecker, W. S. Types of Integration and Their Measurement,
     American Journal of Sociology, Vol. 56, 1950, pp. 332-340.

Landis, L. M. Community and Social Structure. Iowa City, Iowa:
     Department of Sociology, University of Iowa, 1971. Mimeo-
     graphed.

Lansing, J. B. and Kish, L. Family Life Cycles as an Independent
     Variable. American Sociological Review, Vol. 22, October
     1957, pp. 512-519.

_____ and Barth, Nancy. Residential Location and Urban
     Mobility: A Multivariate Analysis. Ann Arbor, Michigan:
     Institute for Social Research, University of Michigan, 1964.

_____ and Marans, Robert. Evaluation of Neighborhood
     Quality, Journal, American Association of Planners, May
     1969, pp. 195-199.

Laumann, E. D. Prestige and Association in an Urban Community. Indianapolis: Bobbs-Merrill Co., 1966.

Lee, Terence. Psychology and Living Space, Transactions of the Bartlett Society, Vol. 3, 1966, pp. 11-36.

_____ Neighborhood as a Socio-Spatial Schema, Human Relations, Vol. 21, 1968, pp. 241-267.

_____ The Psychology of Spatial Orientation, Architectural Association Quaterly, Vol. 1, No. 3, 1969, pp. 11-15.

_____ Perceived Distance as a Function of Direction in the City, Environment and Behavior, Vol. 2, 1970, pp. 40-56.

Lenski, G. Power and Privilege: A Theory of Social Stratification. New York: McGraw Hill, 1966, pp. 30-32.

Logan, M. I. Work-Residence Relationships in the City, Australian Geographical Studies, Vol. 6, 1968, pp. 151-166.

Lowrey, R. Distance Concepts of Urban Residents, Environment and Behavior, Vol. 2, 1970, pp. 52-73.

Lyman, S. M. and Scott, M. B. Territoriality: A Neglected Sociological Dimension, Social Problems, Vol. 15, 1968. pp. 236-248.

Lynch, Kevin. The Image of the City. Cambridge: The MIT Press, 1960.

Maslow, A. H. Motivation and Personality. New York: Harper, 1964.

McKinney, John. Constructive Typology and Social Theory. New York: Appleton Century-Crofts, 1966.

Meeker, B. F. Decisions and Exchange, American Sociological Review, Vol. 36, 1971, pp. 485-495.

Merton, Robert K. On Theoretical Sociology. New York: The Free Press, 1957.

Michelson, William. An Empirical Analysis of Urban Environmental Preference, Journal, American Institute of Planners, December 1966, pp. 355-360.

_____ Man and His Urban Environment. Reading, Massachusetts: Addison-Wesley, 1970.

Miller, Delbert C. Handbook of Research Design and Social
    Measurement. New York: David McKay Company, 1970.

National Academy of Sciences. Moving Behavior and Residential
    Choice. Washington D.C.: Highway Research Board, 1969.

Osgood, Charles E. et. al. The Measurement of Meaning. Urbana,
    Ill: University of Illinois Press, 1967.

Peterson, G. L. A Model of Preference: Quantitative Analysis of
    the Perception of the Visual Appearance of Residential
    Neighborhoods, Journal of Regional Science, Vol. 7, 1967,
    pp. 19-31.

_____ Subjective Measures of Housing Quality, unpublished
    Ph.D. Dissertation. Evanston, Ill.:Northwestern University,
    1965.

Pred, Allan. Behavior and Location. Part I, Studies in Human
    Geography. Lund, Sweden: Department of Geography, Royal
    University of Lund, 1967.

Presteman, D. R. Methods of Assessing Housing Preferences, Forest
    Products Journal, Vol. 70, No. 3, March, 1970, pp. 41-46.

Ramsay, J. O. and Case, B. Attitude Measurement and the Linear
    Model, Psychological Bulletin, Vol. 74, No. 3, 1970, pp.
    185-192.

Ravitz, Mel J. Use of Attitude Survey in Neighborhood Planning,
    Journal, American Institute of Planners, No. 4, 1957, pp.
    179-183.

Rees, H. The Factorial Ecology of Metropolitan Chicago, Master's
    Thesis. Chicago: Department of Geography, University of
    Chicago, 1968.

Robinson, A. Ecological Correlations and the Behavior of
    Individuals, American Sociological Review, Vol. 15, 1950,
    pp. 251-267.

Rokeach, M. The Role of Values in Public Opinion Research,
    Public Opinion Quarterly, Vol. XXXII, Winter 1968-69,

Rossi, P. H. *Why Families Move*. New York: The Free Press, 1955.

Rummel, R. J. *Applied Factor Analysis*. Evanston, Illinois:
    Northwestern University Press, 1970.

Rushton, Gerard. The Scaling of Locational Preferences, in
    Cox,Kevin and Golledge, R. G. (eds). *Behavioral Problems
    in Geography*. Evanston. Illinois: Northwestern University
    Press, 1969, pp. 197-227.

_____ Temporal Changes in Space Preference Structures,
    Proceedings, Association of American Geographers, Vol. 1,
    1969, pp. 129-133.

Saarinen, T. F. Perception of Environment. *Resource Paper* No. 5,
    Commission on College Geography, Association of American
    Geographers, 1969.

Sartain, A. Q. et.al. *Understanding Human Behavior*. New York:
    McGraw Hill, 1958.

Seeley, John et.al. *Crestwood Heights*. New York: Basic Books,
    1956.

Segal, D. R. and Meyer, M. W. The Social Context of Political
    Partisanship, in Dogan, M. and Rokkan, S. (eds).
    Quantitative Ecological Analysis in the Social Sciences,
    Cambridge: The MIT Press, 1969, pp. 217-232.

Shepard, R. N. On Subjectively Optimum Selection Among Multi-
    attribute Alternatives, in Shelly, M. W. et.al. (eds).
    Human Judgment and Optimality. New York: Wiley and Sons,
    1964, pp. 257-281.

Shinn, Allen M. Jr. Measuring the Utility of Housing: Demonstrating
    a Methodological Approach, *Social Science Quarterly*, July
    1972, pp. 88-102.

Smith, M. Brewster. The Personal Setting of Public Opinion in
    Fishbein, Martin (ed)., *Readings in Attitude Theory and
    Measurement*. New York: Wiley and Sons, 1967, pp. 58-69.

Sonquist, John A. *Multivariate Model Building*. Ann Arbor:
    Survey Research Center, University of Michigan, 1971.

Srole, Leo. Social Integration and Certain Corollaries: An
    Exploratory Study, <u>American Sociological Review</u>, Vol. 21,
    No. 6, December 1956, pp. 709-716.

Stegman, M. A. Accessibility Models and Residential Location,
    <u>Journal</u>, American Institute of Planners, Vol. 35, 1969,
    pp. 22-29.

Strauss, Anselm. <u>Images of the American City</u>. New York: The
    Free Press, 1961.

Suits, D. The Use of Dummy Variables in Regression Equations,
    <u>Journal</u>, American Statistical Association, Vol. 52, 1957,
    pp. 548-551.

Tannenbaum, A. S. and Bachman, J. G. Structural Versus Individual
    Effects, <u>American Journal of Sociology</u>, Vol. 69, 1964, pp.
    585-595.

Torgerson, W. S. <u>Theory and Methods of Scaling</u>. New York: Wiley
    and Sons, 1958.

Wachs, M. <u>Evaluation of Engineering Projects Using Perceptions
    of and Preferences for Project Characteristics</u>. Evanston
    Illinois: Transportation Center, Northwestern University,
    1967.

Warner, W. L. <u>et. al</u>. <u>Social Class in America</u>. Chicago: Science
    Research Associates, 1949.

Warren, Roland L. <u>The Community in America</u>. Chicago: Rand McNally
    & Co., 1963.

Webber, M. M. Order in Diversity: Community Without Propinquity,
    in Wingo, Lowdon, <u>Cities and Space</u>. Baltimore: Johns
    Hopkins Press, 1963, pp. 23-54.

Weiss, S. F. <u>et. al</u>. Consumer Preferences in Residential Location,
    <u>Research Previews</u>. Chapel Hill, N.C.: University of North
    Carolina, Vol. 13, 1966, pp. 1-32.

Wilson, R. L. Livability of the City: Attitudes and Urban Develop-
    ment, in Chapin Jr., F. Stuart and Weiss, Shirley F. (eds).
    <u>Urban Growth Dynamics</u>. New York: Wiley and Sons, 1962, pp.
    359-399.

Wind, Yoram. et. al. The Determinants of Vendor Selection: The
Evaluation Function Approach, Journal of Purchasing, Vol.
4, August 1968, pp. 29-41.

_____ Incongruency of Socio-Economic Variables and Buying
Behavior in McDonald, T. R. (ed). Marketing Involvement
in Society and The Economy. Chicago: Proceedings of the
American Marketing Association Educators Conference,
August 1969.

Wittick, R. I. and Horton, F. E. Manual of Computer Programs,
Special Publication, No. 1. Iowa City, Iowa: Department
of Geography, The University of Iowa, October 1968.

Wolpert, J. Migration as an Adjustment to Environmental Stress,
Journal of Social Issues, Vol. XXII, 1966, pp. 92-102.

Zannaras, Georgia. An Empirical Analysis of Urban Neighborhood
Perception. Unpublished Master's Thesis. Columbus:
Department of Geography, Ohio State University, 1968.

Zetterberg, Hans L. On Theory and Verification in Sociology,
Bedminister Press, New York, 1965.

Zimmerman, C. C. The Changing Community. New York: Harper, 1938.

APPENDIX A

THE DATA COLLECTION PROCEDURE AND QUESTIONNAIRE

APPENDIX A

THE DATA COLLECTION PROCEDURE AND QUESTIONNAIRE

The data used in this study was collected by the Central Iowa Regional Planning Commission (CIRPC), Des Moines, Iowa, under the auspices of Mr. T. Urban for a housing and attitude survey. The actual questionnaire was developed with the aid of Mr. Larry Landis, Department of Sociology, Drake University, Des Moines. Mr. Landis collected several scales concerned with measuring the degree of social interaction, participation, stability, security and satisfaction with social and physical surroundings. It should perhaps be emphasized here that the housing and attitude survey of the CIRPC consists of cross-tabulations of the responses with no attempt to establish functional interrelations between the variables. Similarly the development of the theoretical measure of residential satisfaction, although latent in the data, is unique to this research and was not envisaged as a methodological framework for the CIRPC survey, (see Ermuth, 1972).

The final questionnaire, a copy of which is included in this appendix, was in two parts. The first part consists of the respondent's socio-economic characteristics such as age, race, marital status, income, occupation, family size and attributes of

the dwelling unit relating to accessibility, purchase price of
house and social and physical conditions of the residential
environment. The second part consists of a series of attitude
scales, three of which were used to measure residential satisfaction: (1) Local-Cosmopolitan, (2) Anomie and (3) Community
Cohesiveness. Since these were discussed in detail earlier they
need no elaboration.

Geographic Designation of Survey Areas

The area surveyed for this study includes the city of
Des Moines and its four western suburbs. It is assumed that the
suburbs are small enough that residents in those areas are able
to identify with them as 'neighborhoods'. The city of Des Moines,
however, is considered too large. The planning staff of the
CIRPC, therefore, after discussion with the City Planning Department staff, the staff of the Southeast Area Planning Council,
and a seminar with the Information Requirements Committee
established a series of localized survey areas for the city of
Des Moines. The building blocks for these areas are census
tracts. Groupings of the census tracts were decided on the basis
of historically-based communities and on the basis of socio-
economic characteristics (see Figure 7).

The boundaries established, naturally, are often arbitrary.
The particular census tract groups were useful, however, to divide

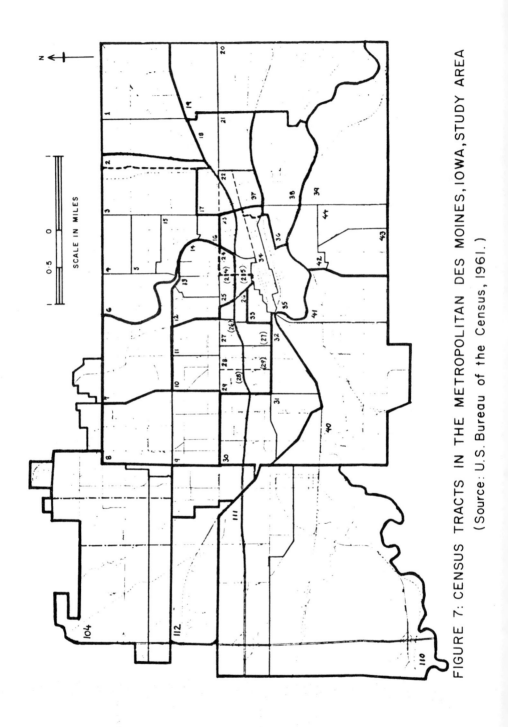

FIGURE 7: CENSUS TRACTS IN THE METROPOLITAN DES MOINES, IOWA, STUDY AREA
(Source: U.S. Bureau of the Census, 1961.)

the city into areas small enough that residents interviewed could base their responses to questions in terms of their 'neighborhood' area rather than the city as a whole.

Selection of Sample

The sample was randomly selected from the Des Moines area telephone directory. The telephone directory was chosen for a base because it is the only source available which includes addresses for all of the areas being surveyed. The City Directory, which would have been a more comprehensive base, includes only the city and three suburbs. It was felt by the CIRPC staff that it was better to have a common survey base for all the survey areas, although the use of the telephone directory eliminated those families without telephones and those persons living in institutional residences such as nursing homes, dormitories, etc.

About 2000 addresses were selected from the directory and then located in census tracts by address. A quota was established for each census tract proportionate to the number of dwelling units in each tract counted in the 1970 CIRPC housing condition survey. Extra addresses were withdrawn randomly and used as a back-up list. Because of time and financial limitations reduced quotas were estalibhsed after the first month of interviewing. For the metropolitan base, an across-the-board 55% of the quota sample was to be used. The total number of interviews completed is 1446.

Interviewing Procedure

Twelve field supervisors were responsible for the training of 65 interviewers for specifically assigned areas. Supervisors were given the lists of addresses for their areas along with assignment sheets, letters of explanation signed by the mayors of each community surveyed, and questionnaires. Interviewers were told to interview the head of the household at each address. If the address was vacant or the household head refused to be interviewed, they were to contact their supervisor for a back-up address. For further specifics regarding the data collection, see Report Number 1, Community Analysis, Central Iowa Regional Planning Commission, July 1971.

NAME _____

ADDRESS _____

PHONE NUMBER _____

CENSUS TRACT _____

COMMUNITY AREA _____

PRE-INTERVIEW CONTACT   Yes _____   No _____

FULL INTERVIEW _____

PROFILE/MAIL OR PICK-UP INTERVIEW _____

CODE # _____ COMMUNITY # _____ C.T.# _____ INTERVIEW # _____

ADDITIONAL COMMENTS OR INFORMATION:

PART I, PROFILE INFORMATION, PAGE 1.

(Questions 1 - 5)

	*Relationship To Household Head	Age	Grades Completed	Sex	Occupation	Location of Job	Race
1							
2							
3							
4							
5							
6							
7							
8							
9							
10							

*   Please include in this list any roomers in the home.

6.   What is the size of the community in which you lived for the longest period of time before you moved to your present home?

Farm or open country	1
Town or village of less than 2500	2
2500 - 9,999	3
10,000 - 49,999	4
50,000 - 99,999	5
100,000 - 999,999	6
One million and over	7

7. How long have you lived in this home?

0 - 3 months	1
3 - 6 months	2
7 months - 1 year	3
1 - 5 years	4
5 years or more	5

8. As closely as you can estimate, please tell me the amount of your household's income from all sources the past year.

$ Under 1,000	1
1,000 - 1,999	2
2,000 - 2,999	3
3,000 - 3,999	4
4,000 - 4,999	5
5,000 - 6,999	6
7,000 - 9,999	7
10,000 - 14,999	8
15,000 and over	9

9. What have you been doing during most of 1970; working, keeping house, going to school, or something else?

Work	1
Looking for Work	2
Keeping House	3
Going to School	4
* Other	5

*Specify other_____

10. What is your marital status?

Married - Civilian (spouse present)	1
Married - Armed Forces (spouse present)	2
Married - Spouse Absent (include separated)	3
Widowed or Divorced	4
Never Married	5

*11. Is this home a:

One Family House	1
Duplex	2
Apartment	3

*12. If apartment, how many units are in the building?_____

Does your home have a:

		Yes	No
13.	Kitchen	1	2
14.	Eating area in the kitchen	1	2
15.	Separate dining room	1	2
16.	Separate living room	1	2
17.	Living-dining room combination	1	2
18.	Family room	1	2
19.	Child's play room	1	2
20.	Utility room	1	2
21.	Basement with finished floors, walls	1	2
22.	Attic with stairs	1	2
23.	Screened or enclosed porch	1	2

24. Bedroom (how many) _____
25. Bathroom (how many) _____
26. Other rooms (specify) _____

Does your home have:

		Yes	No
27.	Electricity	1	2
28.	Running hot water	1	2
29.	Running cold water	1	2
30.	Sewer	1	2
31.	Gas	1	2
32.	Garbage collection	1	2
33.	Flush toilet	1	2

	Yes	No
34. Tub or shower	1	2

35. What kind of heating does your home have?

None	1
Portable	2
Space	3
Central	4
*Other	5

*Specify Other _____

36. What is the extent of the heating in your home?

Only certain rooms	1
All except basement & attic	2
Everything heated	3
Nothing heated	4

37. What kind of fuel do you have?

None	1
Gas	2
Coal	3
Electricity	4
*Other	5

*Specify Other_____

38. Which of the following descriptions best describes the building in which you live?

Building is in need of little or no repair; it is in very good condition.   1

Building needs some repair or maintenance, such as painting, roofing, etc.   2

Building needs major repairs over and above those usually taken care of during normal maintenance, such as rotten window frames, cracks in walls or siding, cracks in foundation, etc.   3

Building is beyond economical repair; walls, roof, porch, etc. are caving in, repairs would be too costly.   4

39. How close to your home is the nearest supermarket?

within walking distance (three blocks)	1
within a short drive (five minutes)	2
within convenient driving distance (15 - 20 minutes)	3
too far away to get to conveniently (over 20 minutes)	4

40. How close to your home is the nearest shopping center?

within walking distance	1
within a short drive	2
within convenient driving distance	3
too far away to get to conveniently	4

41. How close to your home is the nearest park or recreation facility?

within walking distance	1
within a short drive	2
within a convenient driving distance	3
too far away to get to conveniently	4

42. How close to your home is the nearest elementary school?

within walking distance	1
within a short drive	2
within a convenient driving distance	3
too far away to get to conveniently	4

43. How close to your home is the place of employment of the household head?

within walking distance	1
within a short drive	2
within a convenient driving distance	3
too far away to get to conveniently	4

44. If you rent, what is your monthly payment? $_____

45. Does your rent include:

> All utilities (gas, electricity, water) 1
> All except electricity   2
> No utilities   3

46. If you own your home, what is its value? (How much did you pay for it) $_____

47. If you were to sell your home, what do you think you would sell it for? $_____

PART II, ATTITUDE SURVEY, PAGE 7

For the purposes of neighborhood evaluation, you are considered to
be a member of the _____ part of the metropo-
litan area. Please answer the following questions on the basis of
this community area.

Directions: We'd like to have your opinion of a number of
different things. Following is a list of several statements.
As you read each statement, indicate whether you more or less
agree or more or less disagree with it by circling the appropriate number.

	Strongly Agree	Agree	Unsure	Disagree	Strongly Disagree
1. It is more important to have people accept differences than it is to have community agreement.	1	2	3	4	5
2. Time pressures make it awfully difficult for community members to have close personal contacts with one another, even though they would like to.	1	2	3	4	5
3. Considering other responsibilities, there is altogether too much demand on community members to participate in community activities.	1	2	3	4	5
4. It is unfortunate but true that there are very few people around here with whom one can share his interests.	1	2	3	4	5
5. One important way in which people are kept in line around here is through gossip.	1	2	3	4	5

	Strongly Agree	Agree	Unsure	Disagree	Strongly Disagree
6. In our modern world, knowledge must be practical to be meaningful.	1	2	3	4	5
7. Even though they are very competent and conscientious, somehow or other one gets very little stimulation from his neighbors in this community area.	1	2	3	4	5
8. One of the nice things about this community is that the relationships are almost wholly co-operative and friendly.	1	2	3	4	5
9. It is desirable to have a community gathering. This would create a greater degree of agreement among us.	1	2	3	4	5
10. There are too many divisive cliques and groups in this community.	1	2	3	4	5
11. It's hardly fair to bring a child into the world with the way things look for the future.	1	2	3	4	5
12. In spite of what some people say, the lot of the average man is getting worse, not better.	1	2	3	4	5
13. Nowadays, a person has to live pretty much for today and let tomorrow take care of itself.	1	2	3	4	5
14. These days a person doesn't really know who he can count on.	1	2	3	4	5
15. Housing code enforcement is an infringement upon property rights.	1	2	3	4	5

	Strongly Agree	Agree	Unsure	Disagree	Strongly Disagree
16. Building codes are unnecessary; all new residential construction is of good quality.	1	2	3	4	5
17. Only lower class people live in mobile homes.	1	2	3	4	5
18. Property values drop when non-whites move into an all-white neighborhood.	1	2	3	4	5
19. If one non-white and/or low income family moves into a neighborhood, there is the danger that many more will follow, causing suburban ghettos to be created.	1	2	3	4	5
20. Fair housing is not a responsibility of the community area.	1	2	3	4	5
21. There is no housing discrimination in my community area.	1	2	3	4	5
22. Low cost housing projects are unnecessary; there is plenty of older housing for people to live in.	1	2	3	4	5
23. Low income residents will not maintain their property.	1	2	3	4	5
24. People who rent are usually not interested in my community area.	1	2	3	4	5
25. Conflict will almost certainly accompany neighborhood integration.	1	2	3	4	5
26. I feel that my house contributes its fair share to property tax revenues.	1	2	3	4	5

	Strongly Disagree	Agree	Unsure	Disagree	Strongly Disagree
27. People who receive rent supplements do not deserve them; generally they are lazy and taking advantage of the taxpayer.	1	2	3	4	5
28. Fair housing restricts a property owners rights to dispose of his property as he wishes and therefore deprives him of a basic personal freedom.	1	2	3	4	5
29. It is the community's responsibility to provide housing for those families and individuals who can't afford to live in satisfactory housing.	1	2	3	4	5
30. An elected community council is needed to make advisory decisions on housing, zoning, transportation, water, sewer, police, fire, and other public issues to the city council.	1	2	3	4	5
31. Something must be done about air pollution caused by local industry.	1	2	3	4	5
32. Low rent tenant behavior is no different than the behavior of homeowners or higher rent apartment tenants.	1	2	3	4	5
33. A strong tenant's rights organization could best serve the interests of renters who are unaware or unable to protect their rights.	1	2	3	4	5
34. State and local fair housing laws are enforced adequately; there is no need to give enforcement agencies power to fine violators or to compensate a person discriminated against.	1	2	3	4	5

	Strongly Agree	Agree	Unsure	Disagree	Strongly Disagree
35. Multiple dwelling units bring down value of adjoining properties.	1	2	3	4	5

Answer each of the following questions by circling the number of the response that you feel best describes the _____
area or you as a member of that area.

36. Do you feel you are really a part of your area?

    1   Really a part of the area

    2   I am included in most ways

    3   I am included in some ways, but not in others

    4   I don't feel that I really belong

    5   I don't feel that I am really a member of any area

37. If you had a chance to do the same kind of work, for the same pay, in another area within Des Moines, how would you feel about moving from the area in which you now live?

    1   I would very much want to move

    2   I would rather move than to stay where I am now

    3   It would make no difference to me

    4   I would rather stay where I am now than to move

    5   I would want very much to stay where I now live

How do you think the area in which you live compares with the other areas within Des Moines with respect to each of the following points?

38. The way in which the members of the area get along with each other.

    1   Better than most

    2   About the same as most

    3   Not as good as most

    4   I don't know

39. The way in which members of the area stick together.

    1   Better than most

    2   About the same as most

    3   Not as good as most

    3   I don't know

40. The way that the members of the area help each other in their daily lives.

    1   Better than most

    2   About the same as most

    3   Not as good as most

    4   I don't know

Please rate the _____ area on the following characteristics by circling the appropriate response.

	Excellent	Good	Average	Less than Average	Poor
41. Sewers and sewer service available	1	2	3	4	5
42. Separation of pedestrians and vehicles	1	2	3	4	5
43. Quiet streets	1	2	3	4	5
44. Private residential area separate from commercial and industrial nuisances	1	2	3	4	5
45. Natural features: trees, shrubs, grassy areas	1	2	3	4	5
46. Public transportation	1	2	3	4	5

	Excellent	Good	Average	Less than Average	Poor
47. Elementary school nearby	1	2	3	4	5
48. Yards well maintained and free of junk	1	2	3	4	5
49. Street condition	1	2	3	4	5
50. Garbage collection	1	2	3	4	5
51. Public water service	1	2	3	4	5
52. Power supply	1	2	3	4	5
53. Modern education available for every child, youth, and adult	1	2	3	4	5
54. People of different races, sexes, and nationalities have full opportunity to take part in community life	1	2	3	4	5
55. Cultural opportunities: music, art, drama, library service, newspaper, TV, and radio available to the area	1	2	3	4	5
56. Medical and health care readily available to all members of the area	1	2	3	4	5
57. Local government consists of capable citizens who are concerned with community betterment above all	1	2	3	4	5
58. Opportunity through a citizen's council or similar means, for citizens to learn about and take part in area affairs	1	2	3	4	5

59. If you wanted to find out something about housing or housing assistance programs in your area, who would you ask? If possible, please name the person as well as circling the appropriate number.

    1 Mayor_____

    2 School Board Member_____

    3 Local Councilman_____

    4 Area Resident_____

    5 Clergyman_____

    6 Other_____

60. If you wanted to create more effective citizen's participation in your area, who would you choose to organize the area? Again, please name the person if possible.

    1 Mayor_____

    2 School Board Member_____

    3 Local Councilman_____

    4 Area Resident_____

    5 Clergyman_____

    6 Other_____

61. Without being modest, how much influence do you think you have in your area?

    1 More than most people
    2 About the same as most
    3 Very little
    4 None

62. Do one or more of the following places serve as a community center in your area? (Please name it as well as circling the appropriate number.)

    1   Church_____

    2   Shopping Center_____

    3   Community Center_____

    4   Park or recreation facility_____

    5   Other_____

Did you in the past year,	Yes	Unsure	No
63. Inform yourself about issues and problems in the area?	1	2	3
64. Discuss area problems frequently with more than one person?	1	2	3
65. Persuade others to take a particular position on any area issue or problem?	1	2	3
66. Get advice from others with respect to a particular issue or problem?	1	2	3
67. Speak to key leaders about a particular area issue or problem?	1	2	3
68. Visit area organizations or board meetings in an effort to inform yourself about a particular issue or problem?	1	2	3
69. Write letters, or circulate literature, or hold a home meeting about a particular issue or problem?	1	2	3
70. Belong to one or more organizations that takes stands or issues or problems affecting your area?	1	2	3
71. Make group visits or invite visits of local officials to your organization?	1	2	3

The city has developed ahousing code to ensure safe and sanitary housing. Listed below are the code standards for a "decent home."

Enforcement of this code would require property owners to improve, vacate, or demolish housing that does not meet these standards. Do you agree or disagree that these standards are NECESSARY for a decent housing?

	Strongly Agree	Agree	Unsure	Disagree	Strongly Disagree

Every dwelling unit must have:

72. A room or part of a room where food can be cooked.	1	2	3	4	5

If the dwelling unit has a kitchen, the dwelling must have:

73. A kitchen sink in good working order.	1	2	3	4	5
74. Cabinets or shelves for food and dishes.	1	2	3	4	5
75. Stove in good working condition.	1	2	3	4	5
76. Refrigerator in good working condition.	1	2	3	4	5
77. Flush toilet in a private room.	1	2	3	4	5
78. Bathroom sink close to the toilet.	1	2	3	4	5
79. Bathtub or shower which gives privacy.	1	2	3	4	5
80. An exit at least six and a half feet high.	1	2	3	4	5
81. Handrails wherever there are more than four steps.	1	2	3	4	5
82. Safe place to store drugs and poisons.	1	2	3	4	5
83. At least one window or skylight in every room.	1	2	3	4	5
84. The window space in each room should be equal to at least 10 per cent of the total room floor area.	1	2	3	4	5

	Strongly Agree	Agree	Unsure	Disagree	Strongly Disagree
85. At least one electrical outlet or fixture in every room.	1	2	3	4	5
86. Switches placed so that the area ahead is well lighted.	1	2	3	4	5
87. Public halls and stairways well lighted at all times.	1	2	3	4	5
88. A furnace in good working order that can heat every room to at least 70 degrees.	1	2	3	4	5
89. Weather tight, water tight roof, walls, doors, and windows.	1	2	3	4	5
90. Outside wood surfaces protected by paint or other protective covering.	1	2	3	4	5
91. Properly fitted screens on all windows.	1	2	3	4	5
92. Any set of stairs must have steps of equal size.	1	2	3	4	5
93. At least 100 square feet per person living in the dwelling unit.	1	2	3	4	5
94. Ceiling at least seven feet high.	1	2	3	4	5

No one may live in a basement unless:

	Strongly Agree	Agree	Unsure	Disagree	Strongly Disagree
95. Floors and walls are dry year round.	1	2	3	4	5
96. Furnace is separated from the living area by fire resistant insulation.	1	2	3	4	5
97. There are at least two exits, one at least six feet high.	1	2	3	4	5
98. Adequate lighting is provided.	1	2	3	4	5

APPENDIX B

REGRESSION ANALYSES OF RESIDENTIAL SATISFACTION
URBAN ENVIRONMENTAL PREFERENCES
FOR 14 HOUSEHOLD GROUPS

TABLE 17

REGRESSION ANALYSIS[1] OF RESIDENTIAL SATISFACTION
URBAN ENVIRONMENTAL PREFERENCES
CENTRAL HOUSEHOLD GROUP
R = 0.89

Variable Acronym	Beta	F - Value
QUIET	-0.997	31.140
LGSERVIC	0.621	7.701
YARDS	0.531	7.601
ACC2	-0.523	13.224
TRANSP	-0.366	4.309
ACC4	-0.352	1.897
STCONDIT	-0.325	4.609
NATLFEAT	-0.318	6.301
PRIVATE	0.303	3.122
ACC3	0.176	2.410
SEPARATE	0.159	0.684
ACC5	-0.094	0.758
ACC1	0.051	0.168

[1]Analysis of Variance for the Regression: Degrees of freedom are (13,25), computed F - Value = 6.016, significant at the 0.05 level.

TABLE 18

REGRESSION ANALYSIS[1] OF RESIDENTIAL SATISFACTION
URBAN ENVIRONMENTAL PREFERENCES
MODEL CITIES HOUSEHOLD GROUP
R = 0.68

Variable Acronym	Beta	F - Value
YARDS	-0.537	10.737
NATLFEAT	0.251	2.817
ACC4	0.235	3.048
LGSERVIC	-0.207	1.726
TRANSP	-0.084	0.339
ACC2	-0.071	0.246
PRIVATE	-0.066	0.164
ACC3	0.060	0.192
ACC1	0.011	0.006
STCONDIT	0.005	0.001
ACC5	No Data	No Data
SEPARATE	No Data	No Data
QUIET	No Data	No Data

[1]Analysis of Variance for the Regression: Degrees of
Freedom are (8,35), computed F - Value = 3.727, significant at
the 0.05 level.

TABLE   19

REGRESSION ANALYSIS[1] OF RESIDENTIAL SATISFACTION
URBAN ENVIRONMENTAL PREFERENCES
NORTHEAST HOUSEHOLD GROUP
R = 0.70

Variable Acronym	Beta	F - Value
ACC1	-0.637	16.141
ACC2	0.405	7.395
SEPARATE	-0.361	6.036
TRANSP	0.333	5.882
ACC5	0.225	2.984
ACC4	-0.157	1.269
PRIVATE	0.156	0.846
YARDS	-0.094	0.342
NATLFEAT	0.093	0.472
LGSERVIC	-0.090	0.316
ACC3	-0.044	0.106
QUIET	-0.027	0.031
STCONDIT	0.012	0.006

[1]Analysis of Variance for the Regression: Degrees of
freedom are (11,38), computed F-Value = 3.289, significant at
the 0.05 level.

TABLE   20

REGRESSION ANALYSIS[1] OF RESIDENTIAL SATISFACTION
URBAN ENVIRONMENTAL PREFERENCES
HIGHLAND PARK HOUSEHOLD GROUP
R = 0.78

Variable Acronym	Beta	F - Value
SEPARATE	-0.381	12.394
ACC4	-0.264	6.532
TRANSP	-0.263	5.409
PRIVATE	-0.247	5.322
YARDS	0.229	5.003
ACC3	-0.183	4.095
NATLFEAT	0.175	3.334
ACC1	0.150	2.241
STCONDIT	-0.103	0.943
LGSERVIC	0.047	0.155
ACC2	-0.041	0.154
QUIET	-0.027	0.073
ACC5	-0.021	0.063

[1]Analysis of Variance for the Regression: Degrees of
freedom are (13,60), computed F - Value = 7.183, significant at
the 0.05 level.

TABLE 21

REGRESSION ANALYSIS[1] OF RESIDENTIAL SATISFACTION
URBAN ENVIRONMENTAL PREFERENCES
EAST UNIVERSITY HOUSEHOLD GROUP
R = 0.87

Variable Acronym	Beta	F - Value
LGSERVIC	0.687	48.020
TRANSP	-0.543	22.390
YARDS	-0.377	12.391
STCONDIT	-0.337	13.289
ACC2	0.257	6.980
QUIET	-0.168	2.438
NATLFEAT	-0.167	2.558
PRIVATE	-0.158	2.689
ACC1	0.150	2.342
ACC3	-0.107	0.780
ACC4	0.098	0.757
SEPARATE	-0.017	0.026
ACC5	0.006	0.004

[1]Analysis of Variance for the Regression: Degrees of freedom are (12,35), computed F - Value = 9.378, significant at the 0.05 level.

160

TABLE   22

REGRESSION ANALYSIS[1] OF RESIDENTIAL SATISFACTION
URBAN ENVIRONMENTAL PREFERENCES
PARK HOUSEHOLD GROUP
R = 0.81

Variable Acronym	Beta	F - Value
STCONDIT	0.398	1.674
ACC4	-0.314	2.505
ACC1	0.306	1.773
LGSERVIC	-0.290	0.976
PRIVATE	0.281	1.173
QUIET	-0.255	1.352
SEPARATE	-0.247	0.922
ACC5	0.243	2.059
ACC3	0.154	0.787
NATLFEAT	0.151	0.490
TRANSP	0.139	0.153
ACC2	0.078	0.111
YARDS	0.078	0.104

[1]Analysis of Variance for the Regression: Degrees of
Freedom are (13,16), computed F - Value = 2.453, significant at
the 0.05 level.

TABLE   23

REGRESSION ANALYSIS[1] OF RESIDENTIAL SATISFACTION
URBAN ENVIRONMENTAL PREFERENCES
INDIANOLA HOUSEHOLD GROUP
R = 0.67

Variable Acronym	Beta	F - Value
NATLFEAT	0.617	11.123
SEPARATE	-0.366	4.216
LGSERVIC	-0.336	1.871
YARDS	-0.193	0.802
ACC1	0.171	0.984
ACC5	-0.171	0.732
TRANSP	0.144	0.426
ACC3	0.135	0.698
ACC2	-0.083	0.279
STCONDIT	0.064	0.092
PRIVATE	-0.051	0.072
ACC4	-0.026	0.020
QUIET	0.003	0.002

[1] Analysis of Variance for the Regression: Degrees of freedom are (12,28), computed F - Value = 1.927, significant at the 0.05 level.

TABLE   24

REGRESSION ANALYSIS[1] OF RESIDENTIAL SATISFACTION
URBAN ENVIRONMENTAL PREFERENCES
GRAND HOUSEHOLD GROUP
R = 0.74

Variable Acronym	Beta	F - Value
SEPARATE	0.469	11.494
STCONDIT	-0.361	3.331
QUIET	-0.280	2.092
NATLFEAT	0.275	3.424
ACC4	-0.264	3.185
PRIVATE	-0.181	0.943
YARDS	0.160	0.721
ACC2	0.096	0.441
LGSERVIC	0.076	0.138
TRANSP	0.065	0.088
ACC5	0.059	0.169
ACC3	-0.054	0.067
ACC1	0.004	0.001

[1]Analysis of Variance for the Regression: Degrees of
Freedom are (12,27), computed F - Value = 2.707, significant at
the 0.05 level.

163

TABLE   25

REGRESSION ANALYSIS[1] OF RESIDENTIAL SATISFACTION
URBAN ENVIRONMENTAL PREFERENCES
DRAKE HOUSEHOLD GROUP
R = 0.68

Variable Acronym	Beta	F - Value
YARDS	-0.380	12.738
ACC1	0.375	18.731
ACC2	-0.355	15.341
STCONDIT	0.276	6.796
QUIET	-0.275	7.358
LGSERVIC	0.256	3.810
PRIVATE	-0.243	4.838
ACC3	-0.199	6.133
TRANSP	0.117	3.012
ACC4	-0.141	3.748
ACC5	0.071	0.784
NATLFEAT	0.046	0.229
SEPARATE	-0.035	0.144

[1]Analysis of Variance for the Regression: Degrees of Freedom are (13,92), computed F - Value = 6.016, significant at the 0.05 level.

TABLE 26

REGRESSION ANALYSIS[1] OF RESIDENTIAL SATISFACTION
URBAN ENVIRONMENTAL PREFERENCES
MERLE HAY HOUSEHOLD GROUP
R = 0.41

Variable Acronym	Beta	F - Value
ACC3	0.254	4.280
ACC2	-0.228	3.572
ACC1	-0.141	1.496
ACC5	0.136	1.280
SEPARATE	-0.134	0.968
NATLFEAT	-0.120	0.818
ACC4	-0.113	0.846
TRANSP	0.050	0.151
QUIET	0.049	0.159
LGSERVIC	0.048	0.109
STCONDIT	0.030	0.038
YARDS	-0.017	0.015
PRIVATE	-0.014	0.009

[1]Analysis of Variance for the Regression: Degrees of Freedom are (12,68), computed F - Value = 1.149, significant at the 0.05 level.

TABLE 27

REGRESSION ANALYSIS[1] OF RESIDENTIAL SATISFACTION
URBAN ENVIRONMENTAL PREFERENCES
BEAVERDALE HOUSEHOLD GROUP
R = 0.70

Variable Acronym	Beta	F - Value
TRANSP	-0.475	4.004
STCONDIT	0.362	3.754
ACC3	0.316	2.437
PRIVATE	-0.288	1.762
ACC4	-0.276	1.340
ACC5	-0.222	1.912
NATLFEAT	-0.179	0.841
ACC1	0.161	0.888
YARDS	0.145	0.615
ACC2	0.141	0.691
LGSERVIC	0.101	0.149
QUIET	-0.086	0.143
SEPARATE	0.066	0.092

[1] Analysis of Variance for the Regression: Degrees of Freedom are (13,24), computed F - Value = 1.824, significant at the 0.05 level.

TABLE   28

REGRESSION ANALYSIS[1] OF RESIDENTIAL SATISFACTION
URBAN ENVIRONMENTAL PREFERENCES
URBANDALE HOUSEHOLD GROUP
R = 0.78

Variable Acronym	Beta	F - Value
QUIET	-0.344	10.638
ACC4	-0.325	12.696
ACC5	-0.0204	5.311
SEPARATE	-0.180	3.283
YARDS	-0.148	1.283
ACC3	-0.144	2.139
ACC2	0.128	1.650
PRIVATE	-0.106	0.952
NATLFEAT	-0.097	1.233
ACC1	0.046	0.212
LGSERVIC	-0.045	0.163
TRANSP	-0.033	0.114
STCONDIT	0.021	0.038

[1]Analysis of Variance for the Regression: Degrees of
Freedom are (13,61), computed F - Value = 7.129, significant at
the 0.05 level.

TABLE   29

REGRESSION ANALYSIS[1] OF RESIDENTIAL SATISFACTION
URBAN ENVIRONMENTAL PREFERENCES
WEST DES MOINES HOUSEHOLD GROUP
R = 0.56

Variable Acronym	Beta	F - Value
STCONDIT	0.468	10.214
SEPARATE	-0.424	11.286
LGSERVIC	-0.335	3.720
ACC5	-0.310	7.577
PRIVATE	-0.272	4.101
QUIET	0.195	2.065
YARDS	-0.111	0.624
TRANSP	0.093	0.459
ACC3	0.038	0.083
ACC2	-0.032	0.098
ACC1	0.031	0.085
ACC4	-0.017	0.014
NATLFEAT	-0.005	0.001

[1]Analysis of Variance for the Regression: Degrees of Freedom are (12,61), computed F - Value = 2.373, significant at the 0.05 level.

TABLE 30

REGRESSION ANALYSIS[1] OF RESIDENTIAL SATISFACTION
URBAN ENVIRONMENTAL PREFERENCES
WINDSOR-CLIVE HOUSEHOLD GROUP
R = 0.82

Variable Acronym	Beta	F - Value
PRIVATE	-0.451	8.313
ACC4	0.360	5.398
YARDS	-0.340	3.793
ACC3	-0.262	2.449
NATLFEAT	-0.227	1.474
ACC1	-0.164	0.800
TRANSP	0.144	0.751
SEPARATE	-0.130	0.603
LGSERVIC	-0.118	0.312
ACC5	-0.097	0.543
STCONDIT	-0.072	0.172
QUIET	-0.044	0.086
ACC2	-0.040	0.075

[1]Analysis of Variance for the Regression: Degrees of
Freedom are (13,24), computed F - Value = 3.74, significant at
the 0.05 level.

APPENDIX C

REGRESSION ANALYSES OF RESIDENTIAL SATISFACTION
URBAN ENVIRONMENTAL PREFERENCES AND HOUSEHOLD CHARACTERISTICS
FOR 14 HOUSEHOLD GROUPS

TABLE   31

REGRESSION ANALYSIS[1] OF RESIDENTIAL SATISFACTION
URBAN ENVIRONMENTAL PREFERENCES AND HOUSEHOLD CHARACTERISTICS
CENTRAL HOUSEHOLD GROUP
R = 0.95

Variable Acronym	Beta	F - Value
QUIET	-1.336	35.966
YARDS	0.923	15.759
LGSERVIC	0.759	10.026
TRANSP	-0.710	10.186
ACC2	-0.574	11.620
NEWTYPE	-0.542	7.394
NATLFEAT	-0.506	12.229
PRIVATE	0.391	3.688
STCONDIT	-0.316	3.639
SEPARATE	0.277	1.504
LOGSATIS	0.144	1.022
ACC4	-0.219	0.202
NEWSES2	0.099	0.351
ACC5	-0.096	0.411
LOGSES	0.083	0.074
NEWSES1	0.082	0.108
ACC3	0.075	0.252
NEWRACE	-0.068	0.195
LOGFLC	-0.046	0.105
ACC1	0.023	0.021

[1]Analysis of Variance for the Regression: Degrees of
Freedom (24,14), F = 4.98; significant at the 0.01 level.

TABLE   32

REGRESSION ANALYSIS[1] OF RESIDENTIAL SATISFACTION
URBAN ENVIRONMENTAL PREFERENCES AND HOUSEHOLD CHARACTERISTICS
MODEL CITIES HOUSEHOLD GROUP
R = 0.79

Variable[2] Acronym	Beta	F - Value
YARDS	-0.455	6.653
NATLFEAT	0.349	4.282
LOGFLC	0.310	4.359
ACC4	0.246	3.286
NEWSES2	-0.243	1.282
LGSERVIC	-0.239	2.110
LOGSATIS	-0.208	1.458
NEWRACE	0.173	1.121
PRIVATE	-0.171	0.872
TRANSP	-0.168	1.111
LOGSES	0.138	0.399
ACC2	-0.131	0.574

[1]Analysis of variance for the Regression: Degrees of
Freedom (16,27), F = 2.73; significant at the 0.05 level.

[2]Variables not included because F - level insufficient
for further computation: STCONDIT, NEWTYPE, ACC1, ACC3, NEWSES1;
incomplete data for: ACC5, SEPARATE, QUIET.

TABLE 33

REGRESSION ANALYSIS[1] OF RESIDENTIAL SATISFACTION
URBAN ENVIRONMENTAL PREFERENCES AND HOUSEHOLD CHARACTERISTICS
NORTHEAST HOUSEHOLD GROUP
R = 0.84

Variable[2] Acronym	Beta	F - Value
ACC1	-0.602	18.658
NEWSES2	0.480	5.137
LOGSATIS	0.457	11.352
LOGSES	-0.364	1.262
ACC2	0.359	7.216
SEPARATE	-0.295	4.305
LGSERVIC	-0.232	2.162
TRANSP	0.215	2.407
ACC3	-0.172	1.426
ACC4	-0.171	1.429
ACC5	0.142	1.588
PRIVATE	0.128	0.620
NEWSES1	-0.120	0.258
LOGFLC	-0.119	0.835
QUIET	-0.101	0.527
NEWTYPE	0.055	0.154

[1] Analysis of Variance for the Regression: Degrees of Freedom (20,29), F = 3.36; significant at the 0.01 level.

[2] Variables not included because F - level insufficient for further computation: NATLFEAT, YARDS, STCONDIT, NEWRACE.

TABLE   34

REGRESSION ANALYSIS[1] OF RESIDENTIAL SATISFACTION
URBAN ENVIRONMENTAL PREFERENCES AND HOUSEHOLD CHARACTERISTICS
HIGHLAND PARK HOUSEHOLD GROUP
R = 0.83

Variable[2] Acronym	Beta	F - Value
SEPARATE	-0.363	10.522
LOGSES	-0.345	2.420
NEWSES2	0.338	2.766
ACC4	-0.305	7.554
PRIVATE	-0.289	8.473
NEWRACE	-0.268	5.654
YARDS	0.245	5.047
TRANSP	-0.214	3.261
ACC1	0.199	3.612
NATLFEAT	0.191	4.127
ACC3	-0.124	1.652
NEWSES1	-0.118	0.906
LGSERVIC	-0.091	0.447
STCONDIT	0.067	0.296
ACC5	-0.047	0.201
ACC2	-0.047	0.201
LOGFLC	-0.044	0.208
NEWTYPE	-0.019	0.042

[1] Analysis of Variance for the Regression: Degrees of Freedom (23,50), F = 4.86; significant at 0.01 level.

[2] Variables not included because F - level insufficient for further computation: QUIET.

TABLE 35

REGRESSION ANALYSIS[1] OF RESIDENTIAL SATISFACTION
URBAN ENVIRONMENTAL PREFERENCES AND HOUSEHOLD CHARACTERISTICS
EAST UNIVERSITY HOUSEHOLD GROUP
R = 0.90

Variable Acronym	Beta	F - Value
LGSERVIC	0.815	27.053
TRANSP	-0.618	19.204
STCONDIT	-0.347	7.688
YARDS	-0.339	6.092
ACC2	0.249	4.288
NEWSES1	0.243	1.438
QUIET	-0.224	1.967
NEWRACE	-0.160	2.068
ACC1	0.155	1.113
NEWTYPE	0.149	1.685
NATLEFEAT	-0.149	1.129
ACC4	0.143	1.093
PRIVATE	-0.134	1.315
NEWSES2	-0.110	0.384
LOGSES	0.083	0.127
SEPARATE	0.061	0.180
ACC3	0.054	0.103
LOGSATIS	0.052	0.193
LOGFLC	-0.031	0.082
ACC5	0.023	0.045

[1]Analysis of Variance for the Regression: Degrees of Freedom (23,24), F = 4.45; significant at the 0.01 level.

TABLE 36

REGRESSION ANALYSIS[1] OF RESIDENTIAL SATISFACTION
URBAN ENVIRONMENTAL PREFERENCES AND HOUSEHOLD CHARACTERISTICS
PARK HOUSEHOLD GROUP
R = 0.91

Variable[2] Acronym	Beta	F - Value
LOGSES	-0.722	2.321
PRIVATE	0.529	3.768
NEWSES1	-0.497	2.158
QUIET	-0.495	7.825
ACC5	0.469	6.060
TRANSP	-0.393	1.547
NATLFEAT	0.319	2.701
ACC3	0.311	3.348
NEWSES2	0.267	0.445
LOGFLC	0.221	1.539
NEWTYPE	0.196	0.556
STCONDIT	0.178	0.455
ACC1	0.177	0.978
ACC4	-0.106	0.285
SEPARATE	-0.105	0.150

[1]Analysis of Variance for the Regression: Degrees of
Freedom (18,11), F = 3.14; significant at the 0.05 level.

[2]Variables not included because F -level insufficient
for further computation: YARDS, LGSERVIC, ACC2, NEWRACE, LOGSATIS.

TABLE 37

REGRESSION ANALYSIS[1] OF RESIDENTIAL SATISFACTION
URBAN ENVIRONMENTAL PREFERENCES AND HOUSEHOLD CHARACTERISTICS
INDIANOLA HOUSEHOLD GROUP
R = 0.78

Variable[2] Acronym	Beta	F - Value
NATLFEAT	0.634	14.559
YARDS	-0.455	4.607
SEPARATE	-0.398	6.558
LOGSATIS	0.288	2.960
NEWTYPE	0.267	1.712
QUIET	-0.244	1.186
ACC1	0.196	1.647
ACC3	0.186	1.334
ACC4	0.170	0.987
LGSERVIC	-0.159	0.536
PRIVATE	0.148	0.401
TRANSP	0.086	0.185
NEWRACE	-0.008	0.002

[1]Analysis of Variance for the Regression: Degrees of Freedom (16,24), F = 2.35; significant at the 0.05 level.

[2]Variables not included because F - level insufficient for further computation: ACC2, ACC5, ST CONDIT, LOGSES, LOGFLC, NEWSES1, NEWSES2.

TABLE 38

REGRESSION ANALYSIS[1] OF RESIDENTIAL SATISFACTION
URBAN ENVIRONMENTAL PREFERENCES AND HOUSEHOLD CHARACTERISTICS
GRAND HOUSEHOLD GROUP
R = 0.89

Variable[2] Acronym	Beta	F - Value
LOGSATIS	0.505	8.639
ACC5	0.449	6.270
SEPARATE	0.428	6.000
QUIET	-0.334	2.705
LOGSES	0.257	1.243
TRANSP	0.243	1.469
LOGFLC	-0.187	1.354
ACC1	-0.174	0.919
NATLFEAT	0.161	1.134
PRIVATE	-0.149	0.537
NEWTYPE	0.141	0.488
NEWSES2	0.129	0.466
STCONDIT	-0.125	0.368
YARDS	0.124	0.762
NEWSES1	-0.110	0.465
ACC2	0.100	0.400
ACC4	-0.058	0.131
LGSERVIC	0.054	0.110

[1] Analysis of Variance for the Regression: Degrees of Freedom (21,18), F = 3.15; significant at the 0.01 level.

[2] Variables not included because F - level insufficient for further computation: ACC3, NEWRACE.

TABLE 39

REGRESSION ANALYSIS[1] OF RESIDENTIAL SATISFACTION
URBAN ENVIRONMENTAL PREFERENCES AND HOUSEHOLD CHARACTERISTICS
DRAKE HOUSEHOLD GROUP
R = 0.76

Variable Acronym	Beta	F - Value
QUIET	-0.367	12.797
ACC1	0.325	13.774
STCONDIT	0.321	8.999
YARDS	-0.317	8.296
ACC2	-0.282	9.251
LOGSATIS	0.267	7.644
LOGSES	-0.249	4.963
ACC3	-0.224	8.234
PRIVATE	-0.200	3.387
LGSERVIC	0.194	2.042
TRANSP	0.158	2.244
LOGFLC	-0.146	2.998
NEWSES2	0.126	1.546
ACC4	-0.113	1.951
ACC5	0.078	0.877
SEPARATE	-0.067	0.523
NATLFEAT	0.049	0.254
NEWSES1	-0.027	0.082
NEWTYPE	-0.025	0.073
NEWRACE	0.017	0.045

[1]Analysis of Variance for the Regression: Degrees of
Freedom (24,81), F = 4.60 significant at the 0.01 level.

TABLE 40

REGRESSION ANALYSIS[1] OF RESIDENTIAL SATISFACTION
URBAN ENVIRONMENTAL PREFERENCES AND HOUSEHOLD CHARACTERISTICS
MERLE HAY HOUSEHOLD GROUP
R = 0.62

Variable[2] Acronym	Beta	F - Value
LOGSATIS	0.357	8.605
ACC2	-0.257	5.306
ACC1	-0.252	5.360
ACC3	0.248	4.927
ACC5	0.231	4.116
NEWTYPE	0.171	2.709
LOGFLC	-0.168	2.283
LOGSES	0.136	1.297
ACC4	-0.108	0.980
STCONDIT	-0.097	0.599
NEWSES2	0.088	0.557
LGSERVIC	0.081	0.308
TRANSP	-0.048	0.170
PRIVATE	-0.038	0.115

[1] Analysis of Variance for the Regression: Degrees of Freedom (17,63), F = 2.41; significant at the 0.01 level.

[2] Variables not included becasue F - level insufficient for further computation: SEPARATE, QUIET, NATLFEAT, YARDS, NEWRACE, NEWSES1.

TABLE 41

REGRESSION ANALYSIS[1] OF RESIDENTIAL SATISFACTION
URBAN ENVIRONMENTAL PREFERENCES AND HOUSEHOLD CHARACTERISTICS
BEAVERDALE HOUSEHOLD GROUP
R = 0.85

Variable[2] Acronym	Beta	F - Value
TRANSP	-0.772	11.705
LGSERVIC	0.467	2.854
ACC3	0.455	7.534
LOGSATIS	0.384	5.092
SEPARATE	0.253	1.764
PRIVATE	-0.251	1.746
STCONDIT	0.221	1.714
QUIET	-0.201	1.207
YARDS	0.178	1.291
LOGSES	0.121	0.257
ACC4	-0.105	0.245
ACC1	0.100	0.557
NEWTYPE	-0.066	0.213
NEWSES1	-0.059	0.080

[1]Analysis of Variance for the Regression: Degrees of
Freedom (17,20), F = 3.39; significant at the 0.01 level.

[2]Variables not included because F - level insufficient
for further computation: ACC2, ACC5, NATLFEAT, NEWRACE, LOGFLC,
NEWSES2.

TABLE 42

REGRESSION ANALYSIS[1] OF RESIDENTIAL SATISFACTION
URBAN ENVIRONMENTAL PREFERENCES AND HOUSEHOLD CHARACTERISTICS
URBANDALE HOUSEHOLD GROUP
R = 0.82

Variable Acronym	Beta	F - Value
QUIET	-0.356	9.743
ACC4	-0.306	8.833
LOGSATIS	0.234	4.475
ACC2	0.187	2.816
ACC3	-0.184	3.252
YARDS	-0.177	1.593
LOGSES	0.166	1.215
ACC5	-0.141	2.377
SEPARATE	-0.123	1.406
NEWRACE	-0.109	1.143
NATLFEAT	-0.093	0.983
STCONDIT	0.064	0.249
PRIVATE	-0.060	0.258
LOGFLC	0.054	0.262
TRANSP	-0.051	0.272
NEWTYPE	-0.048	0.139
LGSERVIC	-0.046	0.136
ACC1	0.041	0.162
NEWSES2	-0.032	0.092
NEWSES1	-0.031	0.038

[1]Analysis of Variance for the Regression: Degrees of Freedom (22,52), F = 4.92; significant at the 0.01 level.

TABLE 43

REGRESSION ANALYSIS[1] OF RESIDENTIAL SATISFACTION
URBAN ENVIRONMENTAL PREFERENCES AND HOUSEHOLD CHARACTERISTICS
WEST DES MOINES HOUSEHOLD GROUP
R = 0.66

Variable[2] Acronym	Beta	F - Value
STCONDIT	0.471	10.600
SEPARATE	-0.461	10.616
LOGSES	0.372	5.638
ACC5	-0.337	8.231
PRIVATE	-0.288	4.840
LGSERVIC	-0.193	1.283
QUIET	0.176	1.660
NEWRACE	-0.164	1.841
YARDS	-0.160	1.374
NATLFEAT	0.141	1.224
NEWSES1	0.097	0.385
ACC3	0.087	0.601
NEWTYPE	0.077	0.364
LOGSATIS	-0.068	0.293
TRANSP	0.067	0.305
LOGFLC	0.065	0.243

[1] Analysis of Variance for the Regression: Degrees of Freedom (18,55), F= 2.37; significant at the 0.05 level.

[2] Variables not included because F - level insufficient for further computation: NEWSES2, ACC1, ACC2, ACC4.

TABLE 44

REGRESSION ANALYSIS[1] OF RESIDENTIAL SATISFACTION
URBAN ENVIRONMENTAL PREFERENCES AND HOUSEHOLD CHARACTERISTICS
WINDSOR HEIGHTS-CLIVE HOUSEHOLD GROUP
R = 0.91

Variable[2] Acronym	Beta	F - Value
YARDS	-0.421	4.255
ACC4	0.331	3.771
PRIVATE	-0.318	1.857
ACC1	-0.244	1.228
LOGFLC	0.229	1.537
TRANSP	0.213	1.552
ACC3	-0.169	0.884
LGSERVIC	-0.167	0.497
NEWSES1	-0.161	0.452
NEWRACE	-0.155	0.590
ACC5	-0.112	0.520
NATLFEAT	0.111	0.287
LOGSATIS	0.106	0.556
STCONDIT	-0.106	0.298
SEPARATE	-0.081	0.138
LOGSES	-0.057	0.039
NEWSES2	-0.041	0.025
QUIET	0.037	0.044
ACC2	0.037	0.053

[1] Analysis of Variance for the Regression: Degrees of
Freedom (23,14), F = 2.88; significant at the 0.05 level.

[2] Variables not included because F - level insufficient for
further computation: NEWTYPE.

ABSTRACT

Imperfect knowledge of consumer preferences for housing, in general, and the paucity of information on relevant factors involved in residential satisfaction with an urban environment, in specific, promoted this research. The overall objectives are, consequently, to derive empirically valid statements about housing preferences which can form postulates in a theory of residential satisfaction and, ultimately, provide input to our knowledge of residential choice behavior. The statements explicate the preferences of households for social, physical, spatial and esthetic aspects of the residential environment and provide a quantitative-qualitative assessment of current residential satisfaction. They also focus on variations in the socio-economic-demographic characteristics of the households and on variations of attributes of the social and physical environment.

Given a particular housing choice of a household the preferences are assumed to be a function of its perception and evaluation of urban environmental attributes. To replicate the process by which a person integrates information about the stimulus object and makes judgments regarding residential satisfaction with respect to a set of urban environmental attributes an evaluation-function model, originating in psycho-physics, is used. Thus, preferences are derived that are latent in the household's perception responses.

Satisfaction with the residential environment was operationalized, after a rigorous theoretical discussion, in terms of three basic dimensions: social interaction patterns, local territorial identification, and the degree of isolation felt by a household.

To find the appropriate subgroup configurations at which the determinants of residential satisfaction are operative, and to deal with the suspected existence of high-order interactions and non-linearities in the variable relationships, households are aggregated on the basis of commonality of perceptions. This led to the identification of fourteen distinct and relatively homo-geneous perceptial points of view.

The analyses are based on an extensive survey data set of 778 households in metropolitan Des Moines, Iowa. Other contributions of this research may be summarized as follows:

(1) All household groups derive their urban environmental pre-

ferences by essentially the same process of integration and evaluation of attributes of the residential stimulus object. A general
check on the validity of the evaluation-function model, separately
for each household group, is provided by the multiple correlation
coefficients; generally, upwards from 0.75;

(2) Irrespective of group membership households evaluate and
weight relatively few environmental attributes as relevant contributors to residential satisfaction. In general, only between four
and six variables are considered. Based on this empirical evidence
it is concluded that a person confronted with the residential
judgment task can only effectively organize and process these few
factors in the evaluative context;

(3) There are significant spatial variations and, paradoxically,
there is much spatial order in Des Moines in terms of urban environmental preferences. Different levels of the urban environment
(dwelling-unit, residential environment, metropolitan services)
are preferred depending on the location of a household group. In
the city accessibility considerations, public transportation, and
such environmental factors as 'separation of pedestrians and
vehicles' and 'quiet streets' are preferred. In the central city
areas, by contrast, preferences relate more specifically to
improvements in the quality of the immediate housing environment.
In the suburbs residential considerations such as privacy and
esthetic preferences as well as accessibility to work are significant contributors to residential satisfaction;

(4) The addition of socio-economic and demographic household
characteristics, which may be considered as belonging to a
different level in the development sequence, to the modeled functional relationships between residential satisfaction and urban
environmental preferences substantially increased the amount of
'explanation'; generally, around twelve percent.

RESUME

En géneral, la connaisance incomplète des préférences des consommateurs pour le logement et la disette
de ces informations sur les éléments du contentement d'un
milieu urbain, ont avancé cette étude. Par conséquence
on désire dériver des rapports empiriquement valides des
préférences résidentielles. Puis, avec ces informations,
il sera possible de postuler une théorie de la satisfaction résidentielle et enfin, d'augmenter notre connaissance
de la conduite de ceux qui choisissent une résidence.
Les exposés expliquent les préférences des familles pour
les aspects sociaux, physiques, spatiaux, et esthétiques
du milieu et fournissent une courante évaluation qualitative
et quantitative du contentement des résidents. On con-
centre aussi sur les variables dans les traits socio-
économiques, démographiques des ménages et aussi, sur les
variables dans le milieu social et physique.

En choisissant un logement, on présume que les préférences sont une fonction de la perception de ce logement
-là et d'une évaluation des traits dans le milieu urbain.
Pour reproduire la méthode qu'on emploie pour intégrer
les informations sur l'objet stimulant et pour juger le
contentement en fonction des traits du milieu urbain, on
se sert d'un modèle qui dérive de la psycho-physique.
Puis, on dérive des préférences qui sont latentes dans
les réponses perceptuelles du ménage.

La satisfaction du milieu résidentiel est arrivée,
après une discussion théorique, en fonction de trois dimensions: des modèles des relations socialles, l'identification du territoire local, et la solitude qu'éprouve le
ménage.

On peut grouper les ménages en base de la fréquence
des perceptions semblables. Cela mène à l'identification
de quatorze points de vue qui sont distinctifs et assez
homogènes.

Les analyses sont basées sur les résultats d'un
sommaire étendu de 778 ménages dans la ville de Des Moines,
Iowa. On peut résumé sommairement les autres contributions
de ces recherches comme la suivante:

(1)   Toutes les familles tirent leur préférences du
       milieu urbain en employant la même méthode d'intégra-
       tion et d'évaluation des qualités du stimulant

187

résidentiel. On peut vérifier la validité du modèle
"évaluation-fonction" pour chaque ménage en employant
les coefficients de multiples corrélations; en
general, plus de 0.75.

(2)   Indépendant de la composition du groupe, les ménages
évaluent assez peu de qualités du milieu comme des
éléments importants pour la satisfaction résidentielle.
En général, on ne considère qu'entre quatre et six
variables. En employant cette évidence empirique,
on conclut qu'une personne qui a besoin de faire un
jugement résidentiel, ne peut traiter qu'un peu de
ces éléments;

(3)   Il y a des variations significatives dans l'èspace
et, paradoxalement, il y a beaucoup d'ordre dans
l'èspace à Des Moines en fonction des préférences du
milieu urbain.

Les préférences pour les niveaux divers dans le
milieu urbain (le logis, le milieu résidentiel, les
services métropolitains) changent selon l'établisse-
ment du ménage. Dans la grande ville, on préfère
l'accessibilité, le transport public, et des éléments
du milieu tels que "la séparation des piétons et des
autos" et "les rues tranquilles." Aux centres des
grandes villes, par contraste, on s'intéresse plus
spécifiquement à l'amélioration de la qualité du
logement. Dans la banlieue, l'intimité et les préférences esthétiques, de même que l'accessibilité à
l'ouvrage sont assez significatives;

(4)   L'addition des traits socio-économiques et démographiques, qui apportient à un divers étage dans
l'ordre de développement, aux modèles des rapports
fonctionnels entre la satisfaction résidentielle et
les préférences du milieu urbain a augmenté substan-
tiellement la valeur "d'explication"; en général,
environ douze pourcent.

ZUSAMMENFASSUNG

Der Anlass fuer diese Untersuchungen war
unsere unzureichende Kenntnis von den Wohnungs-
anspruechen des Verbrauchers im Allgemeinen, und
im Besonderen der Mangel an Information ueber die
Faktoren die zur Befriedigung der Wohnbeduerfnisse
unter staedtischen Verhaeltnissen beitragen. Das
Haupziel war daher, erfahrungsgemaess gueltige
Feststellungen ueber die Wohnungswahl abzuleiten,
die dann die Grundsaetze einer Theorie der Wohn-
Befriedigung darstellen und schliesslich zu einer
groesseren Kenntnis des Verhaltens bei der Auswahl
der Wohnung fuehren koennten. Diese Feststellungen
erleutern die von Haushalten bevorzugten Wohnungs-
eigenschaften von sozialen, materiellen, raeum-
lichen und aesthetischen Gesichtspunkten her, und
stellen sowohl eine quantitative als auch eine
qualitative Beurteilung der gegebenen Zufriedenheit
mit der Unterkunft dar. Sie sind ausserdem auf die
Unterschiede in den sozial-oekonomischen und
demographischen Eigenschaften des Haushaltes wie
auch auf die der gesellschaftlichen und materiellen
Umgebung gerichtet.

Ausgehend von der Gegebenheit der Wohnungswahl eines Haushaltes wurde die Wahl der bevorzugten
Eigenschaften als eine Funktion der Wahrnehmung
und des Auswertens der allgemeinen staedtischen
Verhaeltnisse betrachtet. Um den Vorgang zu
rekonstruieren durch den Personen Eindruecke ueber
den motivierenden Gegenstand zusammenfassen und
Urteile ueber die Befriedigung der Wohnbeduerfnisse
unter Stadtverhaeltnissen faellen, wird ein
Auswertungs-Funktionsmodell benutzt, welches seinen
Ursprung auf dem Gebiet der Psycho-Physik hat. Auf
diese Weise werden die bevorzugten Eigenschaften
aus den Antworten des Haushaltes abgeleitet.

Nach eingehender theoretischer Besprechung
wurde Zufriedenheit mit der Wohnung mit Hilfe von
drei grundlegenden Dimensionen konkretisiert:
durch die Formen der sozialen Wechselwirkung, die
Identifizierung mit der Nachbarschaft vom territorialen
Gesichtspunkt aus, und durch den empfundenen Grad
der Isolierung.

Um die entsprechenden Kombinationen der
untergeordneten Kategorien zu finden, welche die
Zufriedenheit mit der Wohnung bestimmen, und um
der angenommenen Tatsache von uebergeordneten
Wechselwirkungen und nicht-linearen Variablen
unter verschiedenen Verhaeltnissen gerecht zu
werden, wurden die Haushalte auf der Basis von
gleichen Wahrnehmungen zusammengefasst. Dies
fuehrte zur Identifizierung von vierzehn voneinander
getrennten und relativ homogenen Gesichtspunkten.

Unsere Untersuchungen basieren auf
ausgedehnten Befragungsergebnissen von 778 Haushalten
in Des Moines, Iowa. Andere Beitraege dieser
Untersuchungen koennen wie folgt zusammengefasst
werden:

1)   Die Haushalte aller Kategorien entscheiden
ueber die bevorzugten Eigenschaften ihrer staedtischen
Umgebung durch einen grundsaetzlich gleichen Prozess
der Integration und Auswertung des beobachteten
Wohnungsobjektes. Eine allgemeine Kontrolle des
Bewertungs-Funktionsmodelles wurde an Hand von
vielfachen Korrelations-Koeffizienten fuer jede
Haushaltskategorie getrennt ausgefuehrt; das
Ergebnis lag im allgemeinen ueber 0.75.

2)   Abgesehen von Kategoriezugehoerigkeit bewertet
ein Haushalt relativ wenige Umgebungsfaktoren als
massgebend zur befriedigung des Wohnungsanspruches.
Im allgemeinen werden nur zwischen vier und sechs
Eigenschaften in Betracht gezogen. Aufgrund unseres
Materials ergab sich, dass man, wenn man der
Aufgabe der Wohnungsbeurteilung gegenuebersteht,
nur diese wenigen Faktoren effektiv organisieren
und in dem Auswertungsprozess verarbeiten kann.

3)   Mit Hinsicht auf bevorzugte Eigenschaften
unter Stadtverhaeltnissen gibt es bedeutende
oertliche Unterschiede, aber auch bedeutende
oertliche Regelmaessigkeiten in Des Moines.
Verschiedene Aspekt der Umwelt (die Wohnung selbst,
die unmittelbare Umgebung, oeffentliche Dienste)

werden, je nach oertlichen Lage der Haushalts-
kategorie, unterschiedlich bevorzugt. Im weiteren
Stadtbezirk wurden Gesichtspunkte der Zugaenglich-
keit, der oeffentlichen Transportmittel und
Faktoren wie "Trennung von Fussgaengern und
Fahrzeugen" und 'ruhige Strassen' bevorzugt. In
der Innenstadt sind die Wuensche mehr auf die
Verbesserung der unmittelbaren Wohnungsumwelt
gerichtet. In den Vororten sind Erwaegungen wie
Ungestoertheit, aesthetische Gesichtspunkte und
die Frage der Verbindung zum Arbeitsplatz wichtige
Beitraege zur Zufriedenheit mit dem Wohnsitz.

4)   Die Einbeziehung von sozial-oekonomischen
und demographischen Haushaltscharakteristiken,
die man als zu einem anderen Stadium der Entwick-
lungsfolge gehoerig betrachten kann, erhoehte
den Wert der Ergebnisse bedeutend, im allgemeinen
um etwa zwoelf Prozent.

ABSTRACTO

Los motivos que han promovido esta investigación se pueden
reducir a dos: el conocimiento imperfecto de las preferencias
del consumidor en materia de habitación, en general, y la escasez
de información sobre los factores pertinentes involucrados en
la satisfacción residencial dentro de un ambiente urbano, en
particular. En consecuencia, los objetivos generales son obtener
empíricamente afirmaciones válidas sobre preferencias de vivienda
que puedan establecer postulados para una teoría de satisfacción
residencial y, por último, facilitar una fuerza potencial a
nuestros conocimientos sobre el comportamiento humano cuando se
trata de elegir una residencia. Las afirmaciones explican las
preferencias de la unidad familiar en los aspectos social, físico,
espacial y estético del ambiente residencial, y proveen una
valoración cuantitativo-cualitativa de la actual satisfacción
residencial. Asimismo, enfocan las variaciones en las característi-
ticas sociales, económicas y demográficas de las unidades
familiares, y las variaciones de atributos del ambiente social
y físico.

Teniendo en cuenta una selección de vivienda particular de
una familia, se supone que las preferencias estén en función
de su percepción y evaluación de los atributos ambientales urbanos.
Para repetir el proceso por el que una persona integra la
información sobre el objeto-estímulo y establece criterios
referentes a la satisfacción residencial con respecto a un conjunto
de atributos ambientales urbanos, se utiliza un modelo originado
en la sicofísica basado en la evaluación y funcionalidad. De
este modo emanan preferencias que permanecen latentes en las
respuestas perceptivas de la familia.

Luego de una rigurosa discusión teórica se definió la
satisfacción con el ambiente residencial en términos de tres
dimensiones básicas: patrones de interacción social, indentifi-
cación territorial local, y el grado de aislamiento deseado por
cada familia.

Para determinar las configuraciones de subgrupo apropiadas
en que actúan los determinantes de la satisfacción residencial, y
para tratar con la supuesta existencia de interacciones de alto
nivel y sin vinculación directa con las relaciones variables, se
agrupan las familias sobre la base de las características comunes
de sus percepciones. Esto condujo a la identificación de catorce
distritos y puntos de vista perceptuales relativamente homogéneos.

Los análisis están basados en una serie de datos obtenidos
mediante una amplia investigación de 778 familias en Des Moines,
Iowa, metropolitana. Otras contribuciones de este estudio pueden
resumirse de la siguiente manera:

1º) Todos los grupos familiares establecen sus preferencias
ambientales urbanas mediante el mismo proceso de integración y
evaluación de los atributos del objeto-estímulo residencial. Se
logra una revisión general de la validez del modelo de evaluación-
función, en forma separada para cada grupo familiar, por los
coeficientes de correlación múltiple; generalmente en forma
ascendente a partir de 0.75;

2º) Aparte del número de personas de cada grupo, la familia
evalúa y sopesa relativamente pocos atributos ambientales como
factores contribuyentes relativos a la satisfacción residencial.
En general se consideran sólo de cuatro a seis variables.
Basándose en esta evidencia empírica se concluye que una
persona enfrentada a la tarea de apreciar una residencia sólo
puede organizar y procesar efectivamente estos pocos factores en
el contexto evaluativo;

3º) Hay variaciones espaciales notables y, paradójicamente,
mucho orden espacial en Des Moines en términos de preferencias
ambientales urbanas. Se prefieren diferentes niveles de ambiente
urbano (unidad y ambiente residenciales, y servicios metropoli-
tanos) según la ubicación de un grupo familiar. En la ciudad
se da preferencia a consideraciones de accesibilidad, transporte
público, y factores ambientales como "separación de peatones
y vehículos" y "calles tranquilas". En las áreas centrales de
la ciudad, por el contrario, las preferencias están en función
más específica con las mejoras en la calidad del ambiente
urbano inmediato. En los suburbios se consideran como detalles
importantes para la satisfacción residencial factores como el
aislamiento y las preferencias estéticas, así como la accesibilidad al trabajo;

4º) Al añadir las características socio-económicas y unidades
demográficas, que pueden considerarse como pertenecientes a un
nivel diferente en la secuencia de desarrollo, a una relación
funcional modelada entre la satisfacción residencial y las
preferencias ambientales urbanas, aumentó considerablemente
la cantidad de "explicación" alcanzando, por lo general, hasta
cerca de un doce por ciento.